Secular Sanctity

Edward M. Hays

PAULIST PRESS
New York/Ramsey

Grateful acknowledgement is made to Sign *magazine*
for permission to reprint material that makes up
the chapters entitled "The Prayer of Oneself,"
"The Lost Virtue of Welcoming," and "Simple Emptiness."

Library of Congress Catalog Card Number: 80-80872

ISBN: 0-8091-2314-2

Published by Paulist Press
Editorial Office: 1865 Broadway, New York, N.Y. 10023
Business Office: 545 Island Road, Ramsey, N.J. 07446

Printed and bound in the United States of America

Cover design by Morris Berman
Cover photo by Robert Beckhard

Contents

To Tom Turkle
whose loyalty
sacrifice,
and labor helped
a dream to be born.

Introduction

If you were looking for a guru, you wouldn't choose your local grocer. Few plumbers are spiritual directors and mechanics are not messiahs. These are simple, obvious observations.

Some unknown someone, long, long ago, separated life into two neatly-divided compartments, the spiritual and the material, or the flesh and the spirit. This world and the next world were separated like night and day, as found in the expression "East is East and West is West and never the twain shall meet!" That's why mechanics are never messiahs. The local folk of Nazareth were correct in asking the question about Jesus, "Isn't this the village carpenter?"

Religion and the world live separate lives, since most spiritualities are busily involved with rejecting "this world" in favor of the "next world." The very term "world" implies evil, power, corruption, while the term "spiritual" implies goodness, holiness, and salvation. Naturally, then, these two never intermarry. When Scripture warns that we cannot love God and the world, "the world" means unloving and evil powers, not the ordinary, secular, daily world.

The Latin word for world, "saeculum," is the source of our word "secular." The secular is the direct opposite of the sacred. While the division of the spiritual and the secular has been the historical pattern for many a century, we must ask "Is it still possible in our technological age? Can the spiritual continue to ignore the temporal or treat it as an enemy?"

Once, long ago, in those times, it was possible to turn your back on secular-worldly concerns and go to the desert and be alone with God—to be separated from the secular not for a few weeks but for a lifetime. Entire peoples did this. They rejected "the world," packed up, and went in search of a New Jerusalem. There, wherever they happened to be, they created a separate but holy culture, which was an island of the spiritual in a sea of the secular. We, however, are living in a temporal, secular world and in the midst of a non-religious culture. How, then, do we find a holiness that is whole and also in harmony with all of life? And can we neglect this modern world and still survive? Today, the ultimate catastrophic power is contained in our hands. We cannot reject that reality and seek holiness outside the secular. We cannot walk away from "this world" any more than we can walk away and turn our backs on a small child playing with a loaded pistol! We must find a secular spirituality instead of separating the secular realities from our way to God.

Yesterday's spiritual exercises often are as much out of date as yesterday's weather report. We need a contemporary spiritualilty that has incorporated the spiritual values of past ages with the complex realities of today. We need a modern pathway to holiness that will express our spiritual hungers as well as our secular work. We need a sacred-secular or secular-sacred Liturgy for daily life! We need new prayer forms, new rituals, and even new words to express this harmony of a sacred-secular life. Perhaps we may need some new commandments!

One possible new commandment could be "You shall love the Lord your God with all your heart, with all your soul, and with all your strength, and you shall love the world as yourself!" Keeping this commandment will not be easy, for we will have to learn how to love this temporal world with a total heart. We will have to learn how to love the secular as we love our very selves. Think about it. Is it possible to love machines, computers, dirty laundry, taxes, and all the unspiritual stuff that is a part of our daily life? Can we love our work, our professions, and while doing so, see that this *Love* is also a part of our love for God, the *Divine Mystery*?

When you love something, you take it seriously. We must learn not to neglect but to take seriously our mortgages, nuclear power plants, the use of chemicals, political elections, health care and events on a global scale. We already invest tremendous amounts of energy into these but we see that expression as separate and apart from our love of God and our prayer life. While involved in a secular society, however, we have not lost our taste for the transcendental; we haven't forgotten our hunger for the sacred. But we need help to see the harmony and the holiness in all temporal things.

Churchy language and pulpit vocabulary doesn't help. The patterns of our worship and religious expression do not contain ideas like a holy carburetor, a blessed budget, a sacramental of separation, or a prayer for paying taxes. One way to love the temporal would be to involve it in our ritual, to find ways to sacramentalize it, so we could express it symbolically as part of our way to God. But how?

Jesus, like Buddha and the other holy saviors, lived in the midst of deeply religious cultures. Jesus lived in a society that was overwhelmed with the Presence of God, with the temple, religious ritual and prayer as the central factor of life. Yet, the Carpenter expanded the concept of the spiritual beyond a sacred society to all societies, even a secular society. His Way was that of the temporal, transformed and viewed from the inside, seen as a mystic contemplaive would see it . . . alive with the *Divine Mystery*.

He gives us a pattern for how we can love the world and transform it. At his Last Supper, He takes ordinary, daily things, bread and wine, and while surrounded by ordinary folk, tax-collectors and fishermen, he transforms the secular into the Divine. And why? Why take the temporal and transform it into the

Divine? *Love* was the reason! It was his love for his friends, his love for his Father, and his love for the world that was the reason for Jesus to invest himself totally into the temporal objects of bread and wine. Love has the magic, miraculous power to take the ordinary and to make it extraordinary.

But love the world? The world is too big to love. We mortals can only love that which we can put our hands around or hold in our hands. So this is where we must begin. We take that which fills our hands, our jobs, our work, our daily secular activities and we transform them with love into ourselves! They will still smell like carburetors, still look and sound like IBM machines, but by our loving-prayerful touch, they can become sacraments of ourselves and of our sacred-secular spirituality.

The new saints will be those who by their daily work, in the midst of a temporal technology, will sustain the world and so bring about its salvation. In their work they will find their nourishment as well as their prayer. As the ancient Bhagavad Gita of India says, "Man reaches perfection by his loving devotion to his work."

To be a "new" saint will require knowledge and skill of one's work as well as the heart of an artist and lover. Such a heart is the same as that of a contemplative, since it can see beneath the chrome, steel and grubby realities of life to the internal mysterious presence. With a contemplative awareness, the work of the person becomes his art and his prayer. All work, as the Carpenter from Nazareth taught us, is holy, priestly, sacramental, and worship. This awareness will only be possible if we are faithful to the commandment, "You shall love the Lord with all your heart, with all your soul, and with all your strength . . . and the world as yourself."

Prayerfully Reading

What you are doing at this moment is reading. If you are like most of us, you are in a hurry. Read slowly these instructions on "how to read." But, if you are able to read the instructions, you might say "Why do I need instructions on how to read?" Reading is a truly marvelous ability. It was one of the first skills we learned in grade school. The educational concept was simple but profound. Learn to read and then read to learn. Reading was the key to our entire education, both in school and in daily life.

In the Gospels, we read that Jesus went into the synagogue on Saturday, as was his custom, and that he stood up to read from the scroll of the prophet Isaiah. Like many other things in the Gospels, we can miss the marvels for the miracles. What is intriguing is that the village carpenter of Nazareth even knew how to read. We take that skill as ordinary and not the least

7

unusual for an adult. But even today, in the closing years of the twentieth century, that ability to read is far from ordinary in many parts of this planet. In ancient days, the skill of reading, as well as writing, was an art reserved for the temple priests. Even seven hundred years after Christ, the great emperor Charlemagne could not read or write. The monks that clustered about his throne were more than chaplains. They were his indispensable secretaries.

Today, while schooled in the skill, many people find it difficult to find the time to read. I have a sister-in-law who told me that to find "time" to read demanded planning in her day. I am sure that many of you reading this have found it difficult to arrange your time so that some quiet and peace might be present. To read today for information or pleasure is not necessary, for we receive information and recreation from so many other sources. Messages come to us in a multitude of ways: television, radio, tapes, telephone, motion pictures, books, magazines, satellite communications and even the daily mail. The spiritual implications of these new transistorized sacraments have not yet been fully realized. The prophets of doom have, of course, labeled them as evil and dangerous, yet they can be tools for the construction of a New Jerusalem. Comunications are the construction tools for the advent of the Kingdom.

These new means of communication, that have for many replaced reading, are tools for a New Jerusalem, a new age, because they are shrinking the earth while expanding our personal worlds. Television alone makes us more catholic (universal). For example, during the past 12 years, international television transmissions by satellite have increased from 80 to 13,000 hours a year. Those vast distances that once separated people from one another are shrinking at an unbelievable speed. The events in the lives of peoples on the other side of the world, peoples unknown to our grandparents, are now daily living room experiences. As we take part in this evolutionary miracle, we have to reshape our ideas and attitudes. We now enter into the mystery of good and evil on a global scale. As we do this, we shall need a new and global outlook on life and we will need a new spirituality—a global spirituality.

You are interested in spirituality. If you were not, you would not even be reading this. You, like so many other people, seek some guidance and support for your inner life. As you look around for someone to guide you, the religious marketplace seems filled with those willing to be of service. From the Orient, gurus and spiritual masters of all sizes and shapes offer to be your spiritual director. Bible-packing preachers and faith healers, together with Sunday morning T.V. evangelists, invite you to call upon them for help. With advent zeal, all these promise you direction in your faltering spiritual journey. But if every person who offered was truly competent, if every pastoral person you knew was willing and capable of giving spiritual direction, there would still be not enough directors so that everyone could be personally directed. Yet it seems some guidance is needed. Does not each person need some assistance in his/her pilgrimage to holiness? Perhaps personal, one-to-one direction is not that absolutely necessary, though it may be of great value.

If you believe that the divine mystery is calling you, that the divine mystery is leading you, then God is your guru. As a guru, God is a perfect director since he knows the secret language of your heart. Perhaps you are, at this moment, being guided by your Spiritual Director—God. The primary function of a good spiritual director is simply to help the other listen to his heart. A good director always works himself or herself out of business. Such a director gives to a person the necessary tools so that he or she can be self-directed in the sense that they can follow the voice of the divine mystery by themselves. That voice speaks the messages needed for your personal journey. Down through the ages, there has always been a shortage of good spiritual directors, but there has never been a shortage of messages, only a shortage of those willing to listen. Buddha was a message. Moses was another such message. Jesus is for some of us *the message*, not in microwaves but in flesh and blood. In fact, we have a global history of countless, saintly satellites that have and are beaming "the message" to all who would take the time to listen, for all who take the time to read.

Today these "mystical messages" are interlaced in a web of communications. The average American listens or is a spectator for about 50 hours a week. That is a total of 2,700 hours a year with television making up about eighty percent of that and radio the remaining percent. That same person reads the newspaper for 215 hours a year and books for 175 hours a year. Reading as a skill is declining but still holding its own in a visual-spectator society. We can take heart that books are even being advertised on television! To lose the skill of reading would be more than a cultural loss; it would also be a personal and spiritual loss.

We seldom think or wonder about this skill that we learned in grade school. At this moment, you are recognizing 200 to 300 printed symbols per minute, decoding those symbols into thoughts and ideas at the same flow as a conversation with the writer. A wondrous magical art is reading! Pre-media ages realized the great power in the printed word as an important tool in the religious life. Even today, surrounded as we are by a multitude of electronic message machines, reading remains a primary means for spiritual self-direction. Books, magazines, newspapers and articles can be for us that spiritual director we have been seeking.

The traditional name for such reading has been "spiritual reading." The very use of that term seems to imply that our lives are neatly divided into spiritual and secular. The marvel of the message, Jesus, was the incarnation (God becoming flesh). The incarnation proclaims a fact we have yet to fully live out, simply that the spiritual and the secular have been homogenized into One. Perhaps a better name for this type of reading that will serve as your means of self-direction in your pilgrimage to Wholesomeness is "Organic Reading." Organic = that which is related to growth, to life, to the ultimate purpose of existence, that which is integrated with the primary function of life. Unorganic reading is that hit-and-miss reading that is without a purpose. Unorganic reading is an activity to kill time in the dentist's office or to fill in time until our favorite program appears on television. Unorganic reading looks for no messages. The purpose of organic reading is related to the growth of the total person. Such reading is done with an attitude of mind that is open and constantly vigilant for messages. Unlike informational reading (the type we did in school), this reading does not seek knowledge but rather messages! The purpose and method of organic reading is based on the realization that once you have begun the pilgrimage to holiness, God will guide you with a continuous flow of messages. You are traveling on this pilgrimage to wholesomeness as a cosmic amphibian, as a person both spirit and animal. We nourish the animal part of the amphibian in countless ways. You must also find ways to nourish the inner person and to awaken the intuitive part of the amphibian. Organic reading opens you to messages that can touch the unconscious. You will find such messages only if you are looking for them and only if you are reading the type of material that contains them.

To look for messages in reading is not easy since our training in that skill was for the purpose of acquiring information. Remember the first grade lesson, "learn to read and then read to learn." Organic reading, the reading of this "letter," requires a different style if we are to find and then decode the messages that deal with our inner life.

Here are a few suggestions that may begin a process of thinking that will allow you to create your own techniques. First, it is not necessary to finish what you are reading before moving on to something else. It is not necessary to read only one thing at a time. You can read several writers at the same time. Since you are looking for messages, you may wish to read the material several times. Because you are not reading to meet some deadline, you can (and should) read much slower. You can set a pace that meets your needs—a page a day or a page a month. The speed of your reading should be such that you can leisurely allow yourself time for thought and prayer. Speed reading is actually opposed to organic reading, so your Evelyn Wood skills will be of little value to you in this area. Instead of speed, you need space. You need both inward and outward space (like reading in the bedroom with the door closed to the sounds of television and the playful noise of the children). You need the environment that will allow you to pause in your reading, to consider what you feel. The freedom to pause when something has touched you, to close the book and your eyes, and reflect about what has been illuminated. Ask yourself the question, "What does this mean to me?" Pondering, you wonder how you can integrate the "message" into your daily life. Usually, you are able to receive and integrate only a single message at a time. Too many messages at the same time are not productive to inner growth. This is the main problem with much of modern media: motion pictures, television, and radio. While being extremely powerful stimuli, they do not allow for the person to stop the flow of images and ideas to explore a personal message that has been revealed. At best it seems that these "moving communications" can communicate a single over-riding idea.

The time to stop, the quiet to ponder, and the leisure to expand a message are necessary if your reading is to be prayer and if it is to be organic and your guru.

Since this type of reading is prayer, you must bring to it a sense of non-productivity. For there will be times reading when you will find no messages and no illumination. The words that you read then can be seeds that drop quietly into the unconscious area of the spirit and there sleep dormant for months and perhaps years. To the qualities of time, leisure and quiet, we now add the next quality, patience, if we wish our reading to be our guru. The organic and prayerful reader allows for this process and does not push for productivity. You should take care, however, that there is present within you an environmental openness so that such seeds can always find a fertile home.

Next, it is important to remember that some things we read will be hollow. Not that they lack depth or substance; in fact, it is just the opposite: they are very "heavy" words. The composition of such words is like that of a lead pipe, heavy but hollow. Remembering the old spy movies when messages were often hidden in hollow canes, we lift up these words out of the text. Carefully, we hold them and listen. Since they are hollow, God uses them to hide messages. They contain marvelous messages beyond the scope of the printed idea and even beyond the imagination of the original writer. To our list of necessary qualities to be a good reader, we will now add another quality; a silence of heart is needed to listen for the messages hidden within the messages.

Ideally the pages of reading matter intended to be organic reading should have wide, white margins with ample room for writing. Wide and ample margins allow space to pencil in your own thoughts, reflections, and questions. Underscoring a thought and "fleshing out" an idea with your own thoughts is a way of entering into conversation with the writer. With a pencil as a prayer tool, you can write creatively your own commentary to the text. Now, the book or magazine becomes an extension of you because you have personalized it. To then share it with another, especially if he has the freedom to pencil in comments, only increases its value.

Finally, an important technique in reading is what happens after we have finished reading. An effective way to activate the message is to discuss it with your friends or with someone with whom you share the same spiritual pathway. In that human and seemingly unproductive communion, words take flesh and ideas become reality. As you "mirror" the message you heard in the reading to another person, that message becomes part of you as you express it in your own unique manner. Thoughts and ideas that are shared with others are ideas that are integrated. One of the main goals of organic growth is the "wholesome" person, made possible by the integration of life and ideas.

An excellent question at this point would be, "Where do I find some organic reading material?" Naturally sacred books are the prime containers of cosmic messages. Not only the sacred books of your religion, but all holy books contain truth. However, God is not restricted by copyright laws only to holy books. Any reading can be organic, but usually it will be those books, magazines, or articles that deal with the needs of the inner person, with meditation and prayer. Reading that touches upon justice and peace, social attitudes and behavior, even the advancement of your life vocation is organic. Mindful that cosmic messages are simple in form but profound in meaning, you can look for them also in stories, parables, and even science fiction. The letters of friends can be a marvelous medium for such messages. Organic reading is a reading that leads you closer to your final destination, to a sense of total unity and harmony. If you know where you are going in life, it will not be difficult to choose which reading material will be organic.

The last and most important quality needed if your reading is to be both prayer and spiritual direction is faith. You, like Jesus when he read in the synagogue, must be possessed by a belief that a Compassionate God wishes to speak to you. Such a faith will make you aware that it is not you who are taking a journey to God. Rather, you are being taken by God on a journey and that all necessary "messages" will come to you as you have need of them. With such an awareness, you will not walk in the footsteps of the great spiritual masters but rather you will seek what they sought, making your own path as you follow with faith the personal messages that come to you.

Discipline and Prayer

"Jesus took Peter, John and James and went up a mountain to pray . . ." (Luke 9:28–36).

Why was it necessary to climb up a mountain to find a place for prayer? Wouldn't it have been easier to have prayed in the home of Peter? Why this difficult journey, and this "waste" of time and energy? The answers to such questions are unknown to us, but we can use an armchair sport—speculation—and as we do, explore an aspect of the spiritual life: discipline! Climbing the mountain to pray instead of finding some quiet vineyard that was convenient, if not handy, can be seen as a way to say that prayer is not always handy and convenient. Often prayer seems like climbing a mountain, for it takes time and discipline. For those who reject any discomfort and demand convenience, true prayer will be difficult.

As Americans living in the twentieth century, we

17

delight in convenience in our food, our travel, and in just about every aspect of our lives including prayer. Supermarkets and churches, both anxious to be successful and popular, are making their services as convenient as possible. Yet the very essence of being a disciple is discipline, so much so that the two words are from the same root. These three students in the school of prayer, Peter, John and James, knew that no one can enroll in "that" school of Christ's without being willing to embrace a life of discipline.

The disciples knew that if you wished to be more than simply a believer in Jesus, if you wished to be a disciple of his, you had to accept discipline. For the Master had said, "If you wish to be my disciple, you must deny your very self, take up your cross daily and follow me." There is nothing vague about that requirement or about his other statements that demanded total dedication and a singleness of purpose.

Christianity and Zen are both religions of the will. They uphold intuition above intellection, since intuition is the more direct way of reaching the truth. They appeal to military persons and to athletes because those persons treat life and death with indifference, and their occupations demand a discipline of life. The words of Jesus, "Be on your guard, be awake, be vigilant lest your enemy catch you asleep," are military words. No wonder then that in both the East and the West, we find military type persons drawn to these religions. The Samurai warriors of Japan, the knights of Europe, together with hermits and saints embraced a religion that showed them how to conquer themselves and to find liberation. In the *Dhammapada*, the Buddha says, "It is better to conquer yourself than to win a thousand battles."

Both Zen Buddhism and Mystic Christianity have demanded a sense of discipline and order in life. A routine of prayer and daily tasks is offered that is directed toward the achievement of something that is greater and more universal than the small individual self.

To hope for spiritual progress without a sense of discipline is hopeless, for unless we can say "no" to ourselves, we can never say "yes" to God and to the needs of others. This discipline must be of the heart, not external but internal, and self-willed. Without it, our prayer life will be haphazard and unproductive. And yet, it should not be a surprise to us that people find it difficult to have time to pray or that a request to make sacrifices is greeted with displeasure. As a society we value comfort more than discipline. We seek a "convenience Christianity," an easy spirituality, and as a result, we have also grown lazy and flabby in the spirit.

Returning again to Buddhism, we find a quotation of the Buddha that adds light to the requirements of Jesus, for the Buddha said, "Life is hard for the man who quietly undertakes the way of perfection with purity, detachment and vigor." We tend to shy away from that which is hard and in our soft modern living, we are near danger. Jesus said to us, "Be on your guard lest your spirits become bloated with indulgence and worldly cares. . . ." If today there seems to be little spirit of sacrifice in the lives of people, a reluctance to give of self, could it be that we are "bloated with luxury?" A certain spirit seems to be missing in our churches. There is a dullness present that speaks of an impotence. Should we wonder that few seem inclined to have religious vocations? The enemy of the Spirit is not the diabolic or the communistic, the enemy is the soft life. As the Greek author, Kazantzakis said, we should be vigilant lest our spirits be "smothered to death in lard."

All this talk abut discipline in our prayers and life sounds rather un-American. Such an attitude seems to be contrary to a freedom of heart. If we truly love God, won't our prayers be spontaneous? Doesn't routine in prayer breed a dullness, if not contempt of prayer? Rabbi Abraham Heschel said, "Routine breeds not contempt but attention." Our daily routine of spiritual duties breeds an attention to the inner spirit that might otherwise be asleep or drugged by work and activities. If prayer is present only at meal times and in church, how can we hope to be spiritually strong and free?

Jesus said, "If you make my word your home (if you will live inside my words and be nourished by them) you will indeed be my disciples; you will learn the truth and the truth will make you free." And the crowd became very angry and said, "We are descended from Abraham and we have never been the slaves of anyone; what do you mean, 'you will be made free'?" Like those ancient listeners of Christ who greatly valued their freedom as sons of Abraham, we also tend to resent anyone who implies that we, as Americans, are not free. For America is the land of freedom. "This is a free country, isn't it?" "I can do what I like!" But if our lives lack discipline, we are not free. Oh, we are free to travel where we like, choose the job we prefer, and even marry the person we love, but these are only external freedoms; what about our hearts? Indeed, our external lives can be free but are not our hearts often in bondage because we suffer from addictions of various kinds? And in the lives of so many, there is a rigid conformity of heart and a slavery of spirit. This slavery manifests itself in our lives of addiction. We are addicted to comfort, status, work, having our own way, and unhealthy emotional gratifications.

These statements are not meant to be condemnations of the conveniences that aid us in our homes and work, but we must remember that they are meant to be our servants and not our masters. Just as the intellect has been said to be a good servant but a poor master, so too, the conveniences that are the pride of our society are also poor masters. It is not necessary that we return to some Victorian/Calvinistic discipline. You remember the type, "the do-or-die" style? But it is important that we remember the words of our Lord, "Enter by the narrow gate, since the road that leads to perdition is wide and spacious, and many take it; but it is a narrow gate and a hard road that leads to life, and only a few find it." The *Upanishads* of India express the same thought when they teach that the way is narrow, as narrow as a razor's edge! If we are not to miss the narrow gate, if we are not to slip and fall off the razor's edge, we shall need a discipline in our lives.

As we look for assistance, it would be well to see that the days of external Church laws demanding spiritual perfection are gone. We will be encouraged to holiness but not forced into it. No mother will shake a stick over us demanding that we become holy, not even Holy Mother Church. We must take upon ourselves willingly the discipline of the cross; the Gospels contain more than enough directions for sanctity if we would but live them. And if we choose not to be disciplined, what then? We must be prepared to suffer the consequences.

Suffering is the consequence of a lack of discipline. If we doubt this, one evening spent watching the evening news will give us more than enough examples. Take the modern hostage news story for example. The setting for this news event can be an airliner, a bank, or even a farm house where escaped convicts hold a family hostage. In our modern life, anyone of us could become actors and actresses in this increasingly common experience. The terrorist holds one or more persons hostage, threatening to kill them unless his demands are met. The demands are usually very costly. While the family and police decide what to do, the victim is held prisoner, cut off from those he loves and from all his normal activities. Perhaps one reason why we are so enthralled by this news event is that we have all experienced the same event in our own emotional lives.

Without any warning, in the midst of our activities, we are taken hostage by a terrorist who is ugly, determined, and unwilling to listen to reason. We name this terrorist—greed, anger, pride, jealousy. But under the ski mask, we discover to our horror that his face is our own face! A part of us, an uncontrollable part of us has captured the rest of us. A dark side has risen up and overwhelmed the kind and gentle in us. When this happens, we must exercise discipline and never pay the ransom, never meet the terrorist's unreasonable demands, but rather demand that this terrorist of our heart surrender. If our lives lack discipline, we shall find ourselves frequently being held hostage, and each time we give in to the demands of this experience, we become less free.

The spiritual life is a moral training course that is incomplete without daily prayer, discipline, and spiritual concern. Unless we are willing to embrace such a personal discipline on a daily basis, our dream of holiness will be simply that, a dream.

The Prayer of Oneself

This is a story about the Our Father. As all stories seem to do, it begins many years ago in happy days. In that time, the Our Father lived a comfortable, religious life. He prayed at rosary wakes and was present at both morning and evening prayers. It seemed that he was a perpetual prayer at the times of confessional penance where he usually appeared in sets of three: "Say three Hail Marys and three Our Fathers." He was always an important part of every Mass, whether he was recited or sung. His prayer in Latin rang out strongly, "Pater noster, qui es in caelis ..." Many years ago, he was secure and comfortable, and the Our Father was at peace with his spiritual life. Then came the mid-sixties and its great ground-swell of change. For the past ten years or so, he had begun to experience feelings of doubt about his prayer life. A sense of hollowness and a lack of meaning had become like a shadow that followed him each time he went to pray. Whatever the reason, he now began to pray from a sense of obligation. It was his duty, his responsibility, to pray, but deep within his heart he knew that this could not be a true motive for long. Since at heart he was a deeply spiritual person, he decided that something must be done about his problem with prayer!

He began by reading books on "How to Pray." He read articles and attended conferences—but without success. He made a 30-day Jesuit-directed retreat. While it was an excellent experience, at the end of the 30 days he felt that he still had his problem. Next, he became a member of a Charismatic Prayer Group. He was baptized in the Spirit and even received the gift of tongues; yet it seemed that his prayer life was incomplete. Since the hollowness remained, he now sought out an Indian Guru and became his devoted disciple. Hours on end he would sit in the lotus position and meditate. He stopped eating meat and learned yoga. While feeling a sense of peacefulness in life, he still felt incomplete whenever he went to prayer.

His search for meaning in prayer expanded as he made a Marriage Encounter and then a Cursillo Weekend. These were all to no purpose, as his prayer life remained as barren as the Sahara. So in frustration, like so many others, he completely abandoned praying and became involved in social reform. He marched with the Farm Workers, with Women's Rights groups and joined ecologists at sit-ins at nuclear powerplants.

While doing good and feeling needed, his emptiness at prayer was still part of him. After having tried so many different methods, he finally gave up on methods and simply retreated to the Rocky Mountains. There in a lonely cabin he lived for a year in solitude as a hermit.

The year of solitude came to an end and he began his journey on foot down the mountain. He was aware that his problem with prayer, like a shadow, was still with him, and a great sadness filled his heart. Suddenly, a thunderstorm broke overhead and the rain began to descend like a river. Seeking to escape the downfall, he sought shelter in an old mountain cabin. The cabin was perched on a giant rock beside a roaring mountain stream. It was pale grey with age and in the doorway stood an equally aged old man. The cabin and the man's clothing indicated that he had not found any gold or silver, but his eyes danced with an inner light that revealed he had found a more valuable treasure. The old man welcomed the wet and dripping stranger into his cabin.

The rain-soaked clothing was hanging on the back of a three-legged chair that stood by the wood-burning stove. As he sipped a cup of tea and warmed himself by the stove, the stranger decided that he would share his story of frustration with the old man. He told the old mountain man of his numerous attempts to find a way to pray, his futile attempts at various methods, and even his long years in solitude. At the end of the story, the old man said, "I didn't catch your name, stranger." "My name is 'Our Father' although some call me 'The Lord's Prayer.' " The old man arched his eyebrows like a roller coaster and said, "Why, son, you are prayer. You don't have to learn how to pray. You simply have to be who you are!"

And he continued, "I am a prospector and my trade is to look for gold. But I have learned that there are many kinds of gold. Things like wisdom and truth, as well as those little pieces of yellow rock, are kinds of gold. For the past thirty years, I have searched for gold in that mountain stream out there, and I have also searched in those." With that, he pointed to the other end of the cabin. From the floor to the ceiling there were shelves upon shelves of books. There were books of all sizes and shapes. The old man stood up from his chair by the fire and walked over to the book-lined wall. With care he took down a large, leather-bound volume with a faded letter "A" on its binding. He carried the book back to the stove and opened it to a certain page. He handed it to the man and said, "Here, read this. Perhaps your problem is not one of method, but rather it is something else."

As the rain drummed away on the cabin roof, the weary pilgrim of prayer read, "Aphasis: one of the most serious problems of speech resulting from brain damage or inadequate functioning of the nervous system. This illness shows itself in persons who are unable to speak. The person knows the words he wants to say but cannot negotiate them in speech. Such a person is said to be word-deaf. Aphasia as an illness is caused by an injury to the head. This injury can be a blow or a fall, or perhaps a brain tumor or stroke. The

27

illness can also be congenital." He closed the book and looked perplexed as he handed it back again to the old man.

"You are prayer," said the old prospector. "You are a special and a sacred word of God made flesh. To pronounce your own unique word is to pray the most beautiful, if not holiest, of prayers. You are like the other victims of aphasia. You suffer from the inability to pronounce yourself—to make flesh your own word! Don't feel bad; it is a worldwide sickness and an ancient disease called by a 'fall'. In you, like all the others, it is congenital and passed on at birth."

The old man rose from his chair and poured his guest another cup of tea and continued, "The first word of God made flesh was creation. God said 'sun' and it became flesh—real. And so on with moon, stars, trees, flowers; they became living prayers. Then God thought a most beautiful thought. God spoke the word and the word became flesh—Adam and Eve. They became God's first human prayers made flesh. But then there came this 'fall', this original injury that has been passed down from generation to generation. People became unable to pronounce their own word. They were and they are—word-deaf.

"God doesn't create things; God only creates prayers. Men, women, bugs, grass, birds, and flowers are created prayers of God. All of them, each of them, are inspirations of God made flesh or feather or fin. To learn how to pray is not to learn new and poetic words. To learn how to pray is to learn how to pronounce your own sacred word—to speak yourself! To learn to pray is not to learn some method. It is to know

28

who you are and to be who you are supposed to be. For example, Jesus was a prayerful man, not because he prayed prayers which he did, but because he was a prayer! Jesus was true to the Word that came from his Father, the Word that was himself. In being faithful to who he was supposed to be, he found a cure for the ancient sickness of aphasia. That cure lies in speech therapy and in being true to his word and to your word. Remember, he said, 'Anyone who loves me will be true to my word.' "

There was silence in the old cabin as the stranger thought about what had been said by the old man. Finally he spoke: "I understand, I think, but how do I cure myself of this aphasia?" The old man twisted his white beard in his fingertips and said, "First, you must learn to be quiet both outside and inside. There is so much shouting today and so much noise that folks cannot hear their own special unique words. Everybody seems to be shouting who you should be so loudly that it is difficult to hear for yourself your own special word. A million star-years ago, God whispered in the soul of everyone a sacred and unique word. It continues to vibrate, but oh so softly, so softly! Therefore, your speech therapy must begin with the therapy of no speech—of silence. For only if you are quiet will you hear your own word that resounds within you. You must find quiet places and learn how to be quiet within if you wish to hear your special word.

"The next part of your therapy is learning how to pronounce the word once you hear it. That is the difficult part of the cure, being true to your special personality. You can begin by being grateful for yourself.

You must be deeply thankful that you exist, that the earth is more beautiful, simply by your presence. This part of the cure is most important. You must see yourself as you are—beautiful and good. Everything about the original you is to be seen as good. God does not have bad ideas!"

At this point the old man was leaning closer to his guest. His voice was filled with enthusiasm. "What I mean, stranger, is that you must be able to see everything about you as good—your shyness, your intelligence, your creativity, your physical size, the tone of your voice, the shape of your nose, and even your baldness. There must be no apologies or regrets. You must not wish to be that word or this word, but rather totally accept and be grateful for that unique word of God which is flesh in you! This is a most important part of the cure, for unless you can begin to embrace and be thankful for the word of God made flesh in you, you can never be true to it. You will engage in that destructive wishing of desiring to be some other word."

Again, there was silence in the small cabin. Outside the rain seemed to have stopped, but the grey clouds hung low over the tree tops and thunder rumbled on the other side of the mountain. The old prospector rocked back and forth slowly in his old chair as he watched the face of his guest. Once again, the old man began to speak, "But if you wish to be true to your word, you will have to be strong. Otherwise you will betray your word in the face of the threats and pressures of society. To be true to yourself and who you are supposed to be is perhaps the ultimate responsibility we each have to bear in life. If God has entrusted us with a creative and unique gift and if it is God's will that we be that special word, then we must summon all the power we have to not be forced into some common mold. Speak your own word loudly and with dignity. That is what it means to submit to the will of God. To do the 'Will of God' and to pronounce your own special word, your own special self, is pure prayer. It is also how we pray always, day and night.

"Once you know these things that I have spoken, know them not with your head but with your heart. Then you can read any book and it will be a holy book. Then you can sing any song and it will be a sacred song. For when you are true to your special word and when you are also true to his word, then what Jesus said will be true in your life—that he and the Father will come and make their dwelling place with you, always! Then you don't go to church, you are Church. Then you don't receive the sacraments, you are Sacrament!"

Having said that, the old, white-bearded man was silent. He closed his eyes and rocked silently in his chair. The rain had stopped and now the sun in yellow ribbons fell between the dripping branches of the green pine trees. The guest rose and began to put on his dried clothing. For a long time he stood before the tall Victorian mirror that hung by the cabin door. He stood there in silence looking at himself in that old milk-edged mirror for minutes, or maybe it was for hours. He had no way of knowing how long he had stood there. A profound sense of peace and an abiding sense of communion with God came upon him. It was

31

a peace that was never to leave him again. Still standing in front of the old mirror, he began to speak with conviction and profound prayerfulness: "Our Father who art in heaven, hallowed be your name . . . your kingdom come . . . your will be done. . . ."

The Value of Questioning

In response to a question of how to keep your youth, the author, Ashley Montagu replied, "Well, the trick is very simple—to die young as late as possible!" Hidden within that simple yet profound reply is the art of preserving the spirit of a child. Within the spirit of the child are the expressions of humor, playfulness, and curiosity. The last is the basic human desire to be an explorer. Since the Kingdom of which Jesus spoke was life, it was logical that he would say that only children might enter it—those who die young, at whatever age.

Each year it seems that the preparations for Christmas begin earlier and earlier. Once we were shocked to see signs of Christmas appearing at Thanksgiving time. Halloween now must fight for prime time with Santa Claus. There can be several reasons why we begin to celebrate this ancient winter feast earlier and earlier. Since Christmas is the feast of the Child and of children, we may desire to have more and more of that spirit in our aged of heart and anxious society. Perhaps, in different and creative ways we should celebrate Christmas not from Thanksgiving until December 25th, but from New Year's day until New Year's day. If celebrating Christmas brings out the hidden child within us, then it should be a feast not of 12 days but of 365 days!

Christmas and Christianity are filled with symbols. Visual signs that speak of the invisible include the cross, the dove, the boat, the egg, the lily, the anchor, and the sun and many more. A new symbol for both Christianity and for Christmas, as a festival of youthfulness, would be the question mark. As a new religious symbol, the question mark could be more powerful in our daily lives than the sign of the cross! As a punctuation mark the "?" resembles the " !" and both appear at the end of a line of words. The question mark however has bowed its head in humility and has asked a question instead of making a bold statement. Because the "?" approaches life with the spirit of an explorer, it is the sign of the child and it is a sacred sign. There are two ways to say the simple truth that God is love. We could say, God is love! Or we could say, God is love? The second way opens us up to an entire process of wonder and exploration. The child within would say "How? Why is God love?"

Every child enters life curious, seeking and questioning. With great labor and financial cost, we educate children by eradicating from them this natural passion to question. Education is often that process of remembering and then regurgitating what has been memorized. Education is only one of the social means to smother the eternal child within the heart. Religion also shares in that repression when it makes the question or doubt a sin.

To propose the question mark as the new holy symbol for spiritual people will present some problems, since we have been educated to think of religion as having the answers instead of the questions. A truly great religion does not give answers so much as it raises great questions that challenge the believer to search inwardly for the answers. What is the meaning of life? Where am I going? What do I suffer and what is the meaning of the pain in my life? Are there "pat" answers, easily memorized, to such questions or must each of us struggle within his or her heart to live out the answers? A friend recently sent me a letter that had written across the top of the page a sentence that sounds very Zen. It read, "I owe everything to my teacher, he taught me nothing." Could we in this period of renewed interest in religious education offer a new style of Baltimore Catechism? Like the old Baltimore Catechism, it would be a handbook of religion filled with questions but this new version would not have answers included. Such a teaching tool might once again awaken that natural childlike curiosity within each of us.

Naturally, to question the creeds we have been taught will be a difficult task because of our childhood religious formation. We have been taught that to question was to doubt and to doubt (to even have feelings of doubt) was sinful. Indeed, doubt is part of the mystery of searching, seeking, even seeking the kingdom. As they say in the Orient—doubt leads to questioning, questioning leads to truth and truth leads to enlightenment. That is holiness. To ask questions is part of the prayerful spirituality of any true seeker.

What effect would there be in our lives if our prayers contained more questions? Perhaps we would begin our prayers with the sign of the question, "Lord, am I in communion with you, with all of you, as I begin this prayer?" We could also end our prayers with the sign of the question. "Well, Lord, now that I come to the end of this time of speaking to you, how will you now speak to me in my life?" We could even trace over ourselves the sign of the question instead of the cross when suffering and difficulties, as well as joy, enter our daily lives. Instead of slavish surrender to pain, we ask, "Why and how can I use this experience for glory and for good?" When gifted with joy and blessings, instead of a mechanical "Praise God!" I ask, "Why Lord? Why me? How can I use your gifts with deep gratitude and how can others share in my gifts?" To pray in the sign of the question is to open the gates of heaven because it is to pray as a child.

The question mark is not only the prayer tool of the saint and mystic but also the creative tool of the artist, the genius, the explorer—those persons whom society has been unsuccessful in the suppression of the child within them. Picasso and Einstein share in common with Edison, Columbus and the great mystics, a certain playfulness by which they question, like a child, the assumptions of life. The key to creativity and to saintliness is in remaining open, searching the unknown without fixed assumptions on what one will find. As Matthew Fox says, "We experience the God we belive in, but rather, we should believe in the God we experience." When we search with a question mark as a probing tool our experiences of love, nature, and friendship, we discover God.

The child within us awakens each time we question life in a creative manner (the question mark is not only the holy sign of the child but can also be the poisonous sign of the cynic who viewing life asks the questions, "Is life really worth it? Can anything good come from Nazareth?" Creative questions that come from a youthful heart explore the meaning of persons and experiences. Such a heart is curious about relating these questions to life and discovering something that the heart did not know about itself before. For the young child the question is fun. Like a toy, they play with questions for the fun of it! The spiritual use of the question as a search for holiness should not be devoid of that element of mirth and fun. The presence of mirth is one of the infallible signs of the presence of the *divine mystery*. The question, as a child's toy, is one toy we should possess all our lives because it is an age retardant! As an adult toy, we should carry it to our graves.

This spirit of open-mindedness that is united with a sense of mirth is the means of "dying young as late as possible." In fact the concept of spirit itself is that very childlike quality. To question ourself, life, and God is to be spiritually young and to be spiritually young is to be a mystic. Each of us is called to mysticism, to the daily experience of the *divine mystery*. We will miss that basic human vocation if we are afraid to be curious. We shall also miss that wholeness for which we were designed, that healthy holiness of the children of a holy and healthy God. How many persons die early but have a long wake? Sometimes thirty or forty years pass before they are actually buried when they forget the secrets of staying young. The secrets are to have someone to love, some work for our hands, something to look forward to, and to remain through all of life as childlike explorers, by being persons who think critically.

Not only must we continuously ask questions, but we should learn how to ask the right questions. The use of the question can be a search for an answer or it can be the search for the problem. If we seek a solution to the problem we can easily remain trapped in those tested and tried answers that may be some of the reason why the problem is still around. Searching for the problem is the beginning of the excitement of fresh discoveries and new solutions. A child is usually more concerned with the problem than with finding an answer. We are creative persons when we ask childlike questions. Jesus seemed to frequently question the problem instead of asking a question about the solution or even seeking a solution. That would be natural since he came to announce a New Israel, not to echo the old. His would be a new kingdom with a new attitude of heart and a new solution to aged questions. The Samaritan woman at the well asked him a question, "Our fathers worshiped on this mountain, but you say that at Jerusalem is the place where one ought to worship?" Jesus said to her, "Woman, believe me, the hour is coming when neither on this mountain nor in Jerusalem will you worship the Father" (John 4:20–21). He went on to say that God is a spirit and the persons who wish to worship him must not seek out some building or sacred mountain but rather look within their hearts. They must make those hearts prayerful places of spirit and truth. The question was not where is the true temple but rather what is the temple? The problem was not the geographic place of worship but worship itself.

May our use of the question mark as a religious sign open us to a year-round celebration of being gifted. Gifts come not only on Christmas but daily as we are showered with beautifully wrapped gifts. Some of them are wrapped in sorrow, some in laughter, some in ecstatic joy, some in sweat, and some in confusion. We open these gifts of life with our holy question mark. With it we unwrap some gifts that are very old and some that are very new.

As we began this reflection on the spirit of the child, we said that the question, as a religious sign, could be more powerful than the sign of the cross. Some who read this may have been disturbed by that remark but let them remember that the sign of the cross is the great cosmic question mark. Why? For what reason? Unless we have learned to live as did Jesus, who questioned his life, social customs, environment and religious beliefs, the cross will not ask the most dynamic question of all history. It will be simply a deaf-mute decoration.

Be Where You Are

Recently *Rain* magazine, which advocates simplicity in lifestyle, published a poster that read: "Stop Tourism—Make Where You Are Paradise." The reasons why we take vacations and make use of tourism are numerous, yet it seems that few of the real reasons can best be satisfied by taking a trip. Among the reasons we could list recreation, renewal, relaxation, but these are needs that we should be able to find where we are, at home. "Stop Tourism" is a new movement aimed at the reduction of waste in energy and it is also an effort to reform our local environments. The movement to make "home" more re-creative and relaxing, as well as enjoyable, has to do with the reforming (re-form) of our patterns of life.

Tourism, with its jumbo jets daily flying to paradises named Las Vegas, Tahiti, and other windward islands is a multimillion dollar business. The product that it offers is not travel but the fruits of travel: romance, entertainment, leisure, beauty, and adventure. Every product fills a need and the need that tourism fulfills is the need to get away in order to find what is not present at home. Tourism is but the search for paradise.

What is this paradise that so many millions of people seek? Historically, it finds its beginning in that primeval park where God and humankind lived in harmony. Paradise was God's backyard, a garden filled with every pleasure needed to satisfy the human heart. Paradise, as a scriptural word, meant heaven, the kingdom, life, and the mystical Jerusalem. In Jewish spirituality, the end of the world would be a return to the beginning. We began in paradise and we would return to paradise.

The central theme of the message of Jesus was to re-form (re-shape) your environment, for the kingdom (paradise) was at hand! But to reshape anything requires large amounts of energy and work. To redecorate your home or your heart is time and energy consuming. As a result, it is easier to take a trip to paradise than to make your home into paradise. That we, together with millions of others, pack our bags and turn our backs on home in search of paradise should not be condemned too readily. The search for paradise is a desire that is deeply implanted within our hearts. All of us long for that special place where we will be free to lie in the sun, to wear as little clothing as possible, and to be waited upon by servants . . . "That's paradise." This south sea island dream is but an ancient memory that speaks of our desire to return to the

41

beginning where we and God were living in harmony and peace.

Whether it is an ancient memory or a hidden dream of the heart, tourism seeks to fill a need, the need to get away. We might ask from what, from where? I guess the answer could be from where you are! Where you are can be divided into four places, as if the world were divided into four sections or suburbs. Everyone lives in one of these four places.

Hell is the residence of many people. For them, life is a torture chamber and place of misery, if not punishment. Gehenna, its ancient Jewish name, was a geographical place. It was the valley between Mount Zion and the hills to the south and west. Gehenna was primarily a place where God was not at home. It was hell because God was absent. When God is absent from our lives and our homes, they become hell. Hell is a spiritual world, but its spirits are those of competition, greed, insincerity, and hate. Those who live there live lives that are devoid of the awareness of something greater than themselves. The climate of hell is war between others (with nagging, sniper attacks between persons) and with one's self (a civil war within the heart of the individual). Since God is absent, life is without meaning or purpose. This makes every street in Gehenna a dead end. Hell is also a place of noise and confusion where every discussion becomes an argument. For those persons who live there, vacations are but brief recesses from the raw reality of life. More often than not, when the tourist from hell arrives in his vacation-paradise, he finds that it is hell as well!

Another large group of tourists come from the

section of life called purgatory. For them, life is seen as misery and pain, but the suffering is at least temporary. Someday, somehow, life will be different and they will be happy. They might win a *Reader's Digest* sweepstakes or strike it rich with some unforeseen good luck. Meanwhile, life is meant to be hard work and drab drudgery. Purgatorians grin and bear it, and live out their sentence of existence. They accept the fact that their homes are in purgatory, since life is meant to be a painful cleansing of some past failure or sin. For these people, the idea that someone should enjoy work, prayer, or just living would be inconsistent with the purpose of life on this earth—purgation of their sinful souls. That people are intended by God to enjoy God, their prayers, even their trials and difficulties would strike the purgatorians as most unusual, if not impossible. Since life, from hangnails to hangovers is a place of suffering, the best a person can do is to take two aspirins and go back to work. As tourists, purgatorians usually return home only to experience their grey-edged pain all the more intensely. After a few unsuccessful attempts to find paradise, they prefer to stay home and work even harder while taking more aspirins.

Then we have those persons whose address is limbo. According to theologians of many centuries past, limbo was that place where babies, who died without baptism, were sent. Limbo was neither heaven, hell, nor purgatory, but it was rather a twilight zone between heaven and earth. Limboites are neuter people and are found in all walks of life. For them, living is devoid of adventure, as well as real meaning.

This condition exists because someone has made the major life decisions for them. That someone could be their parents, friends or others, the stars, or simply luck! Since they feel they have had little choice about where they are, they make few personal decisions in life. They follow the crowd and when asked their choice, they usually respond, "It doesn't make any difference to me." However, when limboites say this, they really mean it! They rarely make good tourists, preferring instead to watch television at home. They seldom choose the programs they watch, but simply watch whatever the network gods have decreed for that day. Since they are passive prisoners of life, they rarely, if ever, make any effort to reform it.

"Where do you live?" This is an excellent spiritual question and one that requires a personal answer. Once, as Jesus was walking along a road, two men began to follow him. Turning he asked them what they wanted. They responded, "Where do you live?" He said to them, "Come and see." We are told that they went with him and saw where he lived, and stayed with him (John 1:38). What did these men see when they went home with Jesus? They saw that he did not live in hell, purgatory, nor in limbo, but that he lived in paradise. He lived in God and God lived in him. That relationship of spiritual unity was something that could be felt and seen. The re-forming of life, that Jesus made the central message of his preaching, has its consequences upon our personal environments. Even hell has the possibilities of being re-formed into heaven. If you are unhappy with where you presently live, why not consider re-forming that "where" into paradise?

The message of Jesus was that of the prophets before him. That message was also that of his cousin, John the Baptist and of *Rain* magazine's poster, "Stop Tourism—Make Where You Are Paradise!" If where we are is to become paradise, then we must make God the vital core of that "where." To accomplish this will require from us discipline, effort, and the gift of God's grace. The discipline we will need is that of creating daily space in our lives for prayer and meditation. Both effort and discipline will be required to live in a consciousness that daily life is a ritual of prayer. This liturgy of life is composed of ordinary activities like eating and sleeping, making love, and doing the dishes. This is part of the mystery of praying always. Praying always prevents spiritual tourism. Spiritual tourism, like jumbo-jet tourism, seeks to escape from reality by brief intermissions of peace found in the chapel or at church. Spiritual tourism rejects the reforming of life as possible, or worse yet, rejects it as even part of the divine plan.

Not a single effort to reform your life is wasted effort. The Lord Buddha said, "Better than a thousand words that are useless is one single word that gives peace. Better than a hundred years lived in vice, without contemplation, is one single day of life lived in virtue and in deep contemplation. Better than a hundred years lived in idleness and in weakness is a single day lived with courage and powerful striving." (*The Dhammapada*, Chapter 8) The same theme, central to those who seek to live a spiritual life, is expressed by the Jewish mystic psalmist when he says, "One day within your courts is better than a thousand elsewhere. The threshhold of the house of God I prefer to the dwellings of the wicked" (Ps. 83). If for one day, we can reform where we live, so that it is a place of peace and of harmony, it is a beginning. A beginning, as *The Dhammapada* and the Psalms say, is worth more than a thousand days of stress. We start in small ways by hallowing our homes and our lives in the here and now. A meal prayer, a night blessing, a time for meditation, or even five minutes of silence are means of not going to heaven, but rather bringing down heaven into our homes. We seek a spirituality that does not separate us from life, but rather one that makes every aspect of our common work-a-day lives prayer.

We also should seek ways to make home a place of re-creative energies. Reformation includes exploring ways to enjoy the adventure of life and its unknown, if feared, possibilities. When we take time for re-creation and the enjoyment of life, we are constructing New Jerusalem. Each effort to replace that which is ugly with that which is beautiful, clean, and simple is a living prayer. When we stop rushing around in an attempt to do more and more in less and less time, we are "in prayer." When we attempt to take the busyness out of our business, and allow time to enjoy our work, then it will become paradise, even if only for one day.

Paradise in the here and now is also a place of creative suffering. Jesus said to the thief who hung on the cross next to him, "This day you will be with me in

46

Paradise" (Lk. 23–39). Whenever we struggle to be on the side of Christ in good times and in pain, we are in paradise. To be on his side is to work to create space for re-construction of relationships, for re-modeling of values of our homes and work. To be on the side of Jesus is to be on the side of those who seek to remove discrimination of all types, of those who refuse to engage in competition, exploitation, manipulation and boredom. Then paradise is where you are, because you are where God is! The spiritual path, the "way" is intended only for those who believe that the impossible is possible, that you can make where you are paradise. Those who find this impossible to believe are those who prefer to live elsewhere and are saving their money for tickets to Waikiki.

The Lost Virtue of Welcoming

Not only our home but our hospitality has spiritual aspects. Prayer is possible anywhere and at any time. When we hear the word "prayer," we at once think of church or synagogue. However, the church is but the historical development of the primal church, which is the home. The home or the "domestic church" was the place of prayer, sacrifice, worship, and spiritual life. The parish church or your local church is intended to be the communal gathering of the domestic churches that surround it. When our homes cease to be domestic churches, then the vitality of the local church is short-lived.

Anywhere in the home is proper for prayer, but three places stand out as cardinal points—the table, the bedroom, and the threshold. The first two appear as simply natural, but the third may not at first glance seem that logical. What kind of prayers could you pray at your front door?

The prayer of the front door is one of the most universal and ancient of all prayers and its name is hospitality. Actually, it is more than simple prayer for it is the first sacrament and as such it is worship. We who live in a non-spiritual culture consider the door of a home to be a necessity, but our ancient ancestors considered it as a holy place and a sacred shrine. To believe today that the threshold of your home is a shrine might be considered quaint. To consider the most common, daily actions like saying "hello" and "good-bye" as prayerful and holy deeds would be thought of as odd. Yet, to invite friends to dinner or to receive an invitation to enter another's home is held sacred by all peoples. Or rather, it was held to be sacred prior to our age of progress.

In former ages, people believed that the gods, hidden in disguise, came to visit as strangers. This belief is not restricted to one or two religions, but held by almost all of them. As a result, hospitality was considered as a prime religious requirement. In the Scriptures we find numerous references to the extraordinariness of guests. Abraham, Tobias, Lot and their families entertained guests with honor and respect only to find that they had indeed entertained God! Paul expressed one of the teachings of the early Christian Community on hospitality when he said, "Do not neglect to show hospitality for by that means some have entertained angels without knowing it."

In Jewish spirituality there was a saying: "Hospitality to strangers is greater than reverence for the

49

name of God!" Considering the profound reverence for the name of Yahweh, we can gather how awesome is what happens at the front door. We are familiar with the sound of church bells as a call to prayer and worship. The sound of the doorbell also calls us to prayer, a worship that demands greater reverence than pronouncing the name of God. The doorbell or the knock at the door is indeed a call to prayer and an invitation to the sacrament of care of the stranger. As a sacrament it has cosmic dimensions. The Hebrews, Chinese, Greeks, Romans, and all ancient peoples consider guests as sacred along with the common comings and goings of the family. The doorway or threshold of the home was a holy place, the sanctuary of these daily comings and goings. As such it was protected by a variety of guardian spirits.

On the doorpost of a Jewish home is placed the Mezuzah. In keeping with the command of Moses that the Word of God should be inscribed upon the doorpost of the home, a small box or container is placed there. Inside is a hand-scribed quotation from the Torah which contains the name of God, El-Shaddaei, the All Holy One. This Mezuzah is a protection for the home from evil and a constant reminder of the sacred nature of the threshold. The prayer custom is to touch the Mezuzah and then kiss the fingertips upon entering and leaving the home.

The pre-Christian Romans assigned a special god to guard and bless the doorway and his name was Janus. He had two faces so that he might watch the front and back doors at the same time. The god Janus was the custodian of welcoming and bidding farewell to guests and strangers. As you probably have already guessed, his name was given to the doorway month of the year, January! Those persons who had as their special duty the care of the threshold were called, after his name, janitors, and less common today, janitresses. The janitor was the minister of the sanctuary of the door, not someone who kept the house clean.

According to Moslem spiritual theology, on the day of judgment we must all give a full account of what we have done with the time and money that God has given us. God will demand a full accounting of these two important talents. But, it is said, God will never ask about money or time used in hospitality. So sacred is that action that God would be ashamed to inquire about it. The contemporary person might easily smile at such primitive theology, or the belief that the gods and goddesses come to us as strangers, or that shaking hands is prayerful worship. But remember that our expression "good-bye" is a relic of that age and a reminder of our amnesia about the true nature of hospitality. Once, a long time ago, "good-bye" was said much slower and it sounded like "God be with you."

We also remember that Jesus was a wandering teacher-rabbi and his community had a wandering ministry that made hospitality also a necessity. "Whatsoever you do to the least of my brethren, you do unto me ... I was a stranger and you took me in ..." Each of us then is called to be a janitress or a janitor as we become holy ministers of the threshold. In the words of the early Christian community, "Be generous in offering hospitality." However, the issue

51

was more than hospitality as a necessity for that expression was an important part of a living spirituality. That relationship between hospitality and the inner life remains interlocked even today.

Prayer and the care of guests, of the stranger or friend, are expressions of the divine flow in the universe. Prayer is an awareness, an attitude of remembering, that we are all guests in this world. Prayer is an expression of gratitude for the ways in which we are entertained, gifted and loved by the divine host. Hospitality is but one way to continue the divine flow of gifts through us to others. When we fail to be grateful, to lift up our hearts in gratitude, according to the ancient holy ones, the divine flow ceases. Deeds of kindness and courtesy, of welcoming and friendship, are ways to allow the gifts of life that have come to us to flow on out into the world and for these gifts to return to their original source. Hospitality has implications beyond polite manners because our capacity for receiving is linked to our ability to give. The closed hand and heart that are unable to give love are also unable to receive love.

Within the universe is a stream of divine energy, a sacred flowing of life and love. The divine love is constantly giving itself in an endless stream of daily gifts as God flows out of God and into the world. We discover these flowing gifts in the daily experiences of life by which we are loved. We then pass them onward to others, so that this love might return to its source, the divine heart of God only to begin its journey all over again. This divine flow is mirrored in the cosmic plan within the cycle of rain. Water is constantly moving from the heavens to earth and returning again. Unlike water, the flow of love can stop at the human heart. We can trap the gifts and keep them for ourselves and never pass them on. We each possess the power to close the doors of our hearts and stop the flow. The human heart has a door that closes more easily than it opens. However, the divine flow of gifts freely comes to us and freely it must pass through us on its mystic journey back again to the divine source.

By deeds of hospitality this flowing return of gifts continues as we attempt to love others without seeking profit. As the Teacher said, "When you entertain do not only invite your friends but also the poor and the outcast because they will be unable to repay you by an invitation to their homes." We should seek those opportunities to keep the flow of gifts moving through the universe. Each day we are gifted with expressions of God's love in the beauty of creation that surrounds us and in acts of kindness and affection. We are also provided daily with numerous means of allowing this love to return to its source. Kindness to the stranger can be expressed not only at the threshold of our homes but at the 100,000 other doorways of life. Daily we encounter the stranger (most of whom we may not see again) as clerks in stores, business people and service persons, as well as travelers on the road. In all of these doorways we should be mindful of their sacred natures and also mindful of the divine flow that is on its way back again to God. To stop the flow by closing your heart is to sin. Sin is to stop the divine flow of God's Love and to thereby reject the divine plan of the constant movement of all gifts.

At these countless doorways of life, as well as at your own front door, is found a trinity of the threshold—reverence, love and sincerity. Sincerity is of absolute necessity in hospitality since nothing interrupts the divine flow as does dishonesty. Insincerity is that divorce between what we think or feel and what we say and do. All pretending is alien to true prayer. If we cannot be sincerely kind and reverent, then it is better not to open our front doors. Better that we stay "closed-in" than we act with dishonesty. What better reminder that we have closed the doors of our hearts (unable at this moment to give ourselves to others for various reasons) than to hide behind our closed doors and pretend that we are not at home. That refusal to come to our doors is more honest than to open our doors and pretend that we are courteous and loving. All dishonesty is dangerous, if not lethal, to the growth of the inner life.

Because both love and reverence require time, we should not be surprised at their recent absence from our lives. Today our two most precious possessions are time and money. Should we be surprised that we find a void of prayer and reverence in our homes, if not also hospitality, since we live in a "hurry up" and "rush-rush" society? Being always "busy" prevents other natural virtues, as well, from being present in our homes. To handle with reverence persons and things, we need not only time but also faith, a living belief that a reality, if not *the* reality of all life, does exist beneath the most ordinary and common things.

Time and faith are not sufficient in themselves to

revive love as part of the trinity of the threshold. Love has been replaced in our world not by hate so much as it has been suppressed by fear. We are afraid to be kind to the stranger! We are afraid to exchange the normal courtesy, for in the process we might be robbed or raped. The contemporary news media daily give us a blow-by-blow account of crime and terrorism. This continuous coverage of crime as news has had its deadening effect and what has died is hospitality to the stranger. So easily we forget that for each act of terror there are also 10,000 acts of tenderness (hospitality) that will never find their way into the daily paper or the news program. As a result, welcome mats are rolled up and stored away in the back of the basement. We buy more and more locks for our front doors and sadly, also, for our hearts as well. Tu Fu, a wandering poet of the eighth century in China, expressed his concern at a rebellion in the city of Ch'ang-an by a barbarian general with the lines:

"The rustic old fellow from Shao-ling
weeps with stifled sobs,
as he walks furtively along the bends
of the Serpentine River on a spring day;
In the palaces by the river front
the thousands of doors are locked!
For whom have the fine willows and new rushes
displayed their fresh green colors?"

Has not the fate of the citizens of Ch'ang-an behind their locked doors also become our fate? Has not fear prevented us from experiencing the fine willows as well as the fine people of the world?

Indeed, we all need to be cautious as well as prudent for a growing crime rate is a reality, but so is the presence of God in the stranger a reality. We have a need to control the growing anxiety that feeds our childhood apprehension of the stranger. This growing anxiety which causes us to treat persons like things is fed also by our entertainment. When our entertainment is focused on robbery, murder, and violence, the fear grows. As a result, we today, unlike the ancient ones, see in the stranger not a god but a demon! Somehow we need to rediscover the beauty and grace (spelled also with a capital "g") in hospitality.

The rebirth of the sacrament of hospitality can begin not with the stranger, but among the very persons with whom we live or work. Here in the daily encounters of life, in the comings and goings, in meals and shared activities, we need reverence for each other, sincerity, and love. We need to recapture the mindfulness that expressions like "good morning" and "good night" are prayerful blessings. We need to remember that common actions like opening a door, "fetching" a cool drink and saying "hello" are prayers and sacramental deeds. If we treat all these common family and communal acts as holy, surrounding them with reverence and sincerity, we will never have to fear that we will treat a stranger or guest with disrespect.

We take turns being gifted in life and then gifting others in return. It's a cosmic game—the marvel of God's divine humor that all of life is intended to be a sort of old-fashioned bucket brigade. We are a chain of people and each of us is important as we allow others to fill our buckets with love and then turn and pour our love into the empty bucket next to ours. In such a cosmic chain, everyone is of supreme importance.

The Prayer of Prophets

As we prepare for the year 2000, which is only a few years away, we will find an increasing interest by people in a spiritual activity that might be called prophecy-prayer. The ancient prophet of Israel, Joel, who lived about 2,400 years ago, spoke of a global vocation to prophecy when he said, "Your sons and daughters shall prophesy, your old shall dream dreams, your young shall see visions, and I will pour out my spirit upon all humanity." This vision of the prophet Joel is of a future time when the entire human family is prophetic, instead of a special person or class of people. In our spiritual history the function of the prophet has been to receive the word of God, speak it to the people, and so affirm the basic beliefs and the relation between God and ourselves. Joel's vision of a universal Pentecost was but an expansion of the wish of the great prophet Moses, who said, "I wish that all the Lord's people were prophets and that the Lord would confer His Spirit upon them all!" A beautiful wish from a man upon whom the Divine Spirit had rested in unusual fullness. That wish of Moses and the vision of Joel speak to a personal need of each of us today in these last hours of the twentieth century. Has that global downpour of the Spirit, not upon a special person or some priestly caste but rather upon all the human family, already happened, or are we still waiting for such a cosmic cloudburst?

We associate the future with prophets and seers. Tomorrow, it seemed, was the time frame in which they had the greatest interest. We all are concerned about that point of time—the future, whether it be next week or the next century. Tomorrow and all the tomorrows after it are of great importance to us or we would not spend so much energy and money preparing for that future. After the rapid changes of the past fifteen years, we are anxious about what the next fifteen may bring to us. The owner of the small gas station is concerned about the location of a proposed interstate highway. The farmer is concerned about the price of wheat next year, and the worker wonders if he will have enough retirement money to live in comfort. All of us have an interest in the future. That interest can be about the next century or the next weekend. We watch the long-range forecast of the weather on the evening news with interest, or scan astrological charts in the newspaper. These are modern media prophets who appeal to our primal human desire to know about the future. That interest is growing and book sales reveal our concern. In 1945, only 35 science fiction novels were published (science fiction being those novels that tell us of life in the future), but in 1975 there were 900 such novels printed. That number would even be higher for this year. We are a people in search of what is ahead of us and what we can expect from the future. Preparing for the future is a survival need. In his book, *Future Shock*, Toffler observed, "Under conditions of high-speed change, a democracy (and here instead of 'democracy' you can insert your own name or the word 'family' or 'church' or 'community') without the ability to anticipate condemns itself to death!"

Anticipation is that ability to look forward and to prevent an action in advance. To anticipate in that sense is the work of the religious prophet. Is such a power of anticipation the promised global downpour of the Spirit? With such a gift humanity would not need fortune tellers, psychics, or prophets to help them anticipate the future, for everyone would know how to practice that science.

In our modern society, our prophets are usually not professionally religious persons and are frequently considered to be agnostic. They are usually found not in temples but in arts. They are also found in the ranks of the mentally ill. Poets, writers, artists, and moviemakers attempt to help us anticipate the future by showing a vision of it today. Orwell's book, *1984*, revealed a world in which ordinary people had little or no control of their lives. It was a mythical statement about what is happening today in numerous ways but it was written many years ago. Jules Verne and Buck

Rogers were also prophets. The motion picture of Burgess' *A Clockwork Orange* shocked audiences with its senseless violence, which only six years later was commonplace evening news. The prophetic statements of such artists usually go unheard and we can wonder about the reason for our inability to respond to their warnings.

Patients in our mental hospitals and in the waiting rooms of their psychologists also predict the future. These persons do so by living out consciously what the rest of us are able to keep unconscious, that is, at least for today! The psychosomatically sick members of our society, for certain reasons, have less resistance to the approaching emotional stresses of daily life and so fall victim today to those stresses. The patients, who today are emotionally sick with certain psychological problems as a result of the conflicts of daily life, are predicting in their personal struggles the affliction that will, in years to come, break out on all sides in our society. The mentally ill are the prophets of tomorrow as are the poets, painters, and film makers, for they also tell us what to anticipate. The present common anxiety about the future and about the meaning of life is a common possession of vast numbers of people that first appeared in mental patients in the late 1930's and early 1940's. We can wonder if the emotional problems of loneliness and self-isolation of today's mental patients will, in the year 2000, be household afflictions like the common cold.

Prophets, painters, and mental patients should act like social alarm clocks to awaken us to what is happening in order that we might change our life patterns and values. But the jangling alarm bell runs down and we continue to live asleep, unable to see the future of our families, our marriages, or religious communities. We close our ears and eyes to these prophetic alarms because we have the ability to blind ourselves to those aspects of life that are beyond our control. We block out from our consciousness the continuous flow of prophecies because the Coming Apocalypse seems to be beyond our personal control. But the future of our marriage, our family, or even our own personal future does not lie in the year 2000. That future is being created by us today, here and now, in the midst of our daily lives.

Contrary to common belief, it was the life of "today" that was of the most concern to the ancient religious prophets. Only if the people hardened their hearts today to the message of life would the ugly tomorrow of fire, smoke, and destruction become a reality. The anxiety of our everchanging age should awaken us to prayer, the prayer of the prophets—anticipation! We are also called to live out the anticipation of the prophets—prayer!

Prophetic prayer is the ability to see, not to foresee. It is simply to see today in a clear and realisitc manner. If I do not wish to become a victim of tomorrow, in the words of *Future Shock*, "condemning myself to death," then I must learn to pause, taking time to look closely at my life and what is happening to me today. The prophet playwright Eugene Ionesco in his play *The Bald Soprano* reveals the result of a failure to pause and look closely at life. In his play, a man and woman happen to meet and engage in polite conversation. As they visit, they discover that they both came down to New York from New Haven that morning on the same 10 o'clock train. As they visit, they also discover that they are staying at the same address on Fifth Avenue and that they also both have a seven-year-old daughter. Suddenly they discover they are man and wife! Ionesco's husband and wife did not suddenly become strangers to one another on that 10 o'clock train from New Haven. Their failure to anticipate the gradual separation between them is not unique. How many husbands and wives live lives that prevent them from truly knowing one another because of their excessive involvement in their children? How many religious, in the name of service, live lives that lead to making them strangers within their own communities? Such isolation is the result of a failure to anticipate what life will be like when the children are grown and gone or what life will be like when we are retired and unable to lose ourselves in work. We are all intended to be prophets, persons extremely concerned about the quality of life today. Such persons know that tomorrow is but the total of a thousand todays. If today my life is unhappy, without meaning or purpose, why will tomorrow be anything other than a monstrous emptiness?

Unless I am able to take time this day to pause and look at my life, I shall not be able to anticipate the future. The name of that pause for anticipation is prayer: "If you invoke me and pray to me, I will listen to you; when you seek me, you shall find me; if you search with all your heart, I will let you find me, says the Lord" (Jer. 29:13–14). The prayer of the prophet, then, is not some crystal ball with which to see the future, but rather the ability to see more clearly the present. Seek the present, which is life, with all your heart and do so with the confidence of being gifted with the fullness of life. As prophetic people, the task is not to foresee the tomorrows of 2001, but to enable that tomorrow to come into being. We are creating the year 2001 by enabling the sort of life and relationships we wish to experience at that future time—enabling them to come into existence by work and effort in the midst of our today.

Those persons who can take (or is that "steal"?) time daily to see clearly their lives and relationships will find happiness in the future. We have a certain fascination with fortune-tellers and with psychic predictors. What we need is the same fascination with the condition and quality of today. The future looms beneath the horizon with horrible predictions of overpopulation, of the earth-melting heat of nuclear toys, of the ozone eating SSTs and of our lives controlled by the government with its police force of computers. Personally, we wonder and fearfully consider our own apocalypse. Perhaps this could be in a nursing home staring at a blank wall with mind and body heavily tranquilized, or struggling to survive on a limited income while paying $100 for a pair of shoes we could have purchased in 1978 for only $15, or wondering if we will be alone, without anyone to love us and care for us as we sit behind our triple-locked door and barred windows seeking safety from the violence and terrorism of society. Whatever the future, Jesus continuously told us not to worry about tomorrow. "So do not be anxious about tomorrow; tomorrow will look after itself" (Matt. 6:34). Yes, tomorrow will look after itself if we look after today.

That attitude toward the future requires a good deal of faith and prayer. First, we need the faith to believe that our tomorrows are indeed made from the "stuff" of today; secondly, the practice of prayer which gives the ability to see clearly what is the "stuff" of which our todays are constructed. Are we really too busy to pray, to take time to be still, or do we keep busy so as *not* to look at the "stuff" of our todays? If tomorrow for us is to be a promised land, we will need faith, prayer, and a spirit of spontaneity that will allow us to move freely with whatever is happening. In Japanese poetry there is a form called Haiku which is a brief three-line poem. The ancient master, Kohyo, expressed in three lines what all these words have attempted to say:

The dragonfly
Perches on the stick
Raised to strike him.

The dragonfly, like the prophet, is super-alert. The dragonfly has realized the situation with keen insight. How can the person with the flyswatter kill the dragonfly if it is sitting on the flyswatter? The dragonfly is preserving its life by acting spontaneously. We need to sit in such alertness, which is the basic condition for prophetic prayer. We must, as Jesus said, "watch and pray." Is peace and an experience of the fullness of God a future quality of life for which we are willing to set aside ten minutes each day for stillness and quiet prayer? Ten minutes a day is so little time out of so many hours to sit like a dragonfly on the flyswatter—still, quiet, and watching.

We cannot prepare for the future by stocks and bonds, or by insurance policies or ironclad securities, but only by learning to live today, fully alive and alert. Retirement plans and bank accounts can only assist us to survive, but sitting like Kohyo's dragonfly can show us how to truly live now and in the future.

Death and Discipline

Among the numerous duties of a disciple, two are essential: to embrace a discipline in life not only in theory, but also in daily practice, and to fall in love with death! That is, to be constantly ready to die at any moment and to be willing to sacrifice oneself whenever necessary. The first of these two duties—discipline—while sounding unpleasant and difficult, is not unreasonable. We are aware that even in the lives of great athletes and musicians there is a requirement for long hours of practice and drill, so discipline for saints is reasonable. But the second duty, the eagerness to die, is madness!

"The man who loves his life loses it," said Jesus, and we can rephrase the line, "while the man who hates his life" to read "while the man who loves death" will preserve his life! But to love death sounds devilish because we have been trained from early childhood to love our life and protect it. The paradox is, nevertheless, that unless we can have a love for death, we shall be unable to truly love life.

When we listen to the words of Christ, we find that death and dying are interlaced continuously with his philosophy of life. In his invitation to follow him, he sums up this theme when he says, "If anyone wishes to come after me, let him deny himself . . . for he who would save his life will lose it, but he who loses his life for my sake will find it" (Matt. 16:24–26). Our modern religious motivation is centered in the celebration of life and abounds in themes like resurrection, joy, new life, and being born again. We seldom hear about death and its necessity (its essential necessity) for resurrection! The subject of death, like its twin, discipline, is untouchable in our society. This is not a new manifestation—the result of the reforms of the Second Vatican Council, or permissive parents—it has been around for a long time. In fact, the Irish have an old expression about themselves that goes, "The Irish would rather die than talk about death." What is new, however, is our manner of dealing with the fear of death. Instead of taboos, superstitions, the rituals dealing with the dead, we who live today handle our fears by silence and denial. Rollo May has said that for us, death is pornography; it is the unmentionable dirty word!

Strangers, then, in our midst are the disciples of Christ, for to be a disciple of him who called himself life is to keep the thought of death before our minds day and night. If we keep the reality of death before our eyes daily, as the disciples, we would then be able to discharge our duties in a faithful manner, and being alert spiritually, we would be able to avoid a multitude of disasters in our lives. None of us should take today for granted! Each day must be lived as if it were the last day, and so it is lived with respect and with great enjoyment. Beware of the thought, "I will live a long life." Such thinking is indeed dangerous since it breeds indulgence and gives excuse to dissipate our energy. Such thinking allows the postponing of holiness and growth until tomorrow. "Be constantly on the watch! Stay awake! You do not know when the appointed time will come!" (Mk. 13:33–37). Are these words of a Western gunslinger or a Samurai warrior? They sound like it, don't they? We know whose words they really are, and we can consider the reality of how such words are lived out each time we see a crucifix.

So, we are invited to a love affair with death. We await the "appointed time" as we await the arrival of a special letter from a good friend, with expectation! Such watchfulness has the power to alert talents and skills that would normally require training to bring them into perfection. A Zen story speaks about this mystery.

Once a long time ago in Japan, there was a great swordsman who finally became a teacher in the art of swordsmanship. His name was Ta'ji'ma-nokami. One day there came to him a young man who was a guard at the palace of the shogun, the military governor. The man wished to become a student under the Zen master and to learn the art of swordsmanship. But the old master said to him "As I observe, you seem to be a master of the art yourself; pray tell me, to what school do you belong before we enter into the relationship of teacher and pupil?" But the man replied, "I am ashamed to confess that I have never learned the art." At this the Zen master became very disturbed thinking that the man was attempting to fool him. It was apparent to his skilled eye that this young man who stood before him requesting training was already a master. But the man only denied again that he had ever studied the art of swordsmanship and said that he had no intention of making a fool of the teacher. To this, the sword master replied, "If you say so, then it must be true; but still I am sure that you are master of something, although I do not know what it is." The young man answered by saying, "Yes, if you insist, I will tell you. When I was a boy, I dreamed of becoming a samurai, a great warrior, and I realized that if this was my dream then I must never have any fear of death. Since those first days, I have grappled with death until it is no longer an issue. Death ceases to worry me. May this be what you are referring to?" And Ta'ji'ma' jumped up and exclaimed, "Exactly, that is what I mean. I am glad that I made no mistake in my judgment. For the ultimate secrets of swordsmanship also lie in being released from the thought of death. I have trained hundreds of my pupils along this line, but so far none of them really deserve the final certificate for swordsmanship. You are in need of no technical training, young man, you are already a master!"

The young man was a master because he had been freed from the thought of death (meaning the fearful thought) as he himself said, "Death ceases to worry me!" Like this person, we shall become a master of life when we have been liberated from the fear of death. Then our spiritual powers will bloom into fullness as we walk in the footsteps of the Lord of life who himself balanced life and death with a holy indifference. "Do not be afraid of those who kill the body but cannot kill the soul" (Matthew 10:23). This indifference to death is but another form of the skill and art of poverty, of detachment. Fear of death is a thought, an attitude of the mind, and as such, it is a possession that can be given away. Like other possessions that limit life, when it is given away, we are free to perform wonderful deeds! You will consider every day of your life precious, and, this being so, you will extend yourself beyond the limitations of "this life" while at the same time, tremendous energy will rush into your daily life allowing you to take it seriously. The result is the ability to separate the essentials of life from the non-essentials, and that is at the heart of poverty and simplicity. For as Jesus said, "Life is a greater thing than food and the body more than clothing" (Lk. 12:23).

A love of death and a love of simplicity are in reality the same love. When we let go of hanging on to persons or possessions, we are experiencing an act of dying. Such letting go of attachments is not a penance but a liberation. If we know what is essential in life, the process is not that difficult. There is a story about a very holy rabbi that may show the point. Some people from the United States were traveling in Poland. As they passed through a certain village they were told that in it there lived a very holy rabbi who had

71

made the village his home for most of his life. So the people came to see the holy man and upon entering his home, they were struck by the starkness of the dwelling. A simple sleeping mat, a table, and a bench at which the rabbi sat studying the Scriptures, were the only furnishings that could be seen. The visitors said, "Rabbi, where is your furniture?" And he, looking up from his reading, said, "Where is *your* furniture?" And they answered, "Our furniture, why should we have any furniture with us, we are only passing through here!" And the rabbi replied, "Well, so am I!"

When we are able to die to "things," to be freed from our attachments, we will know how much "furniture" to carry with us as we are passing through life. We will not make the mistake of burdening ourselves with anything that is unnecessary. Together with a certain freedom we will also find that our enjoyment of life will have greatly increased. We will be able to take delight in simple things—a shared cup of tea, a fresh morning sunrise, the first signs of spring, or a conversation with a friend. All these and many others will suddenly be illuminated with splendor from within once they are labeled, "for today only!" Freedom and splendor from within will be joined by appreciation and gratitude in making all of life a joyful experience. But without a mindfulness of death, these essential qualities will be absent. Death, and its companions—separation, loss, retirement, old age, the appearance of gray hairs and wrinkles in our skin—these are a holy mystery. Death and old age are not problems to be solved, they are mysteries akin to the divine mystery, and as such, they require not a problem/solution but rather, a life response.

If we desire to make a wholehearted response to death and to life, we shall, like the man who dreamed of being a samurai warrior, have to learn how to grapple, hand-to-hand, with the mystery of death. But we shall have to be cautious so as not to become insensitive by overexposure to death in the media—the nightly viewing of death in national and international disasters. And with courage, we shall wrestle with death as it enters our personal lives in the death of friends and members of our families. With sensitivity and courage, we will also learn to reverence death as we encounter it in nature—in the plants that die and in the experiencing of the cycles of winter and spring. The news of death should call for a response of reverence if not awe and wonderment. For if we meet the holy mystery of death in these ways, we need not fear that we shall become co-conspirators in the crime of the denial of death.

Life and death, like opposing powers, pull separately at each of our arms. We are pulled apart by the tension of these two mighty mysteries. We become like the strings of a musical instrument, which, when the tension is correct, begins to vibrate with a divine music. But if we deny death, and fearfully shut it out of our lives, the polarity is lost and there is no creative tension. Without tension there is no music, and where there is no music, there is boredom. Being bored with life is an increasingly prevalent sickness. Bored people, who are also boring people, seek more and more stimulants to cure their sickness. And so, our lives when we have refused to have a love affair with death. For people who cannot love death, tragically, if not ironically, cannot love life either.

Work: Prehistoric Prayer

In Walt Disney's original version of "Snow White," there is a charming scene where the Seven Dwarfs are trooping off to work. With picks and shovels on their shoulders, they march along single file singing, "Hi Ho, Hi Ho, it's off to work we go!" Whistling a happy melody, they begin their day. As children, perhaps, we felt that it would be so much fun to go off to work each day. But as we grew older and "work" became necessary for our livelihood, it was no longer looked upon as fun. Work was work and play was fun! Thus began that lifelong struggle between the demands of work and the desire for play.

As adults, a large part of our day is spent in work and not in play. We do not only have to make our daily bread, which doesn't grow on trees, but we must perform numerous tasks in the process of daily living that are also work—eating, dusting, caring for clothes,

75

making our beds. Often, especially in our work-oriented society, these tasks are even more than work; they are chores that we dislike.

Even though work is important to us (Webster's dictionary has 41 different listings under the word "work"), we often spend much time trying to escape from it! We may secretly dream of becoming a millionaire so we can pay others to do our work. We may dream of winning some $100,000 sweepstake with the realization that then we could retire and live in luxury (implication being that we would not have to work). Work can easily become a total way of life for us. We can easily turn everything from our daily living habits to our profession into "work." We can make a "project" out of everything, even brushing our teeth. In a society where our identification is linked to our work, that connection is much easier than we might think. Work is the curse of the sin of Adam. But is it really a curse?

Adam, our first parent, who didn't have to worry about doing any laundry, could be a patron saint for workers in a technological society. The writer of the Book of Genesis tells us: "The Lord God took the man (Adam) and put him in the garden of Eden to till it and care for it." Work, therefore, existed before the famous fall of Adam and Eve. After the fall, the natural act of work became a drudgery, but work itself is not a curse for the sin of Adam. Was Adam made to work, or was work one of the numerous gifts from our most generous God? If so, how was it a gift? Adam was occupied with the work of caring for his garden, which also happened to be God's garden, Eden. Here we have the first clue. His work was part of a much larger and more cosmic plan. His work was also done in communion with his Creator. Here it appears that Adam was also the first contemplative in our Western tradition, because he worked and lived in communion with his Creator. We do not find a single reference to Adam praying. Interesting, eh? The reason we do not is because Adam *was* prayer. His life was so intimately lived in harmony with creation, with the animals and plants, and with his Creator, that everything was prayer. Adam was the first person to "pray always."

We are the great-great-great grandchildren of Adam and Eve, and as a result, we have also inherited, perhaps as part of our DNA code, that vocation to be contemplatives. We, too, should seek a lifestyle where our labor is our prayer, as well as all of life being prayer. George Bernard Shaw once wrote, "The purpose of saints is not to edify us but to shame us!" The purpose of Adam, as the first saint, is to shame us into making our lives a harmony as was his and Eve's. We cannot leave our work, even simple household chores, out of our prayer lives and call ourselves people who pray always. But how do we make our work, our daily activity, prayer?

First, we must attempt to enter into communion with what we do. We do this first by focusing our attention on the work of our hands. We discipline ourselves not to do two things at the same time. Try this and you will find it to be the most difficult of all forms of asceticism. If we are digging a ditch, we dig the ditch and we do not let our minds work at something other than digging. The same with sweeping the floor, washing the dishes, or taking a bath. A single-ness of attention is essential for our work to be prayer-ful and enjoyable. Resist the efforts of the mind to be somewhere else, to be in the future or the past. Live in the present moment and bring to that moment a keen sense of appreciation for what is happening.

Next, we seek a communion with the "stuff" of our work. We respect and reverence the wood, food, information, people, steel, or whatever is the material of our work as we seek a communion with it. As we work in harmony with whatever touches our hands, we also see it as part of a cosmic continuation of creation. Like Adam, we are working with God, even in the most seemingly un-Godlike action. We work in harmony with time and do not try to "force" it to meet our needs. Adam lacked a pocket for a watch and followed a different style of time. As a result of having sunrise and sunset as key points in his day, he did not feel "rushed" to finish. Hurrying or rushing makes a sense of communion difficult. We must limit our activities so that we can do them with a sense of non-hurry. Most people today are overworked, but that doesn't have to be the case. By learning to say "no" to others, to ourselves, perhaps to our compulsive need for accomplishment (to prove ourselves to others, or even to ourselves), we can limit the demands upon us.

Also, in his tilling the garden, Adam found a "part" of his identity but not the totality of that identity. What made Adam important was that he was Adam, and not the kind of work that he did. The same is true for any contemplative. Their importance is because they are daughters or sons of God, not because of any title or job they do.

Next, we should strive to see that our work is a gift. Adam was living in paradise, yet he worked! God gifted Adam with work so that he might sense his harmony in the divine design. Work is a marvelous opportunity for us to build our well-being. By work, we develop a relationship between ourselves and others and between ourselves and our talents. Work is a beautiful discipline for our little and limited egos. When we work with others and with creation, we must deal with our constant desire to be "in charge." Here was the place where Adam and Eve met their downfall; they desired not to be in harmony but to be in charge! Work with others forces us to control our need for constant self-centeredness. Work, like food, is essential for health of mind, body, and spirit. But if our work is to nourish us (as it did for Christ, for he said that his food was to do the work of the Father), it will need to be balanced with that other human activity of play or leisure. As Adam found a "part" of who he was in his work in the garden, we will also find a part of ourselves in our work. The other part is found in play. It is not impossible that our work can also be fun. In a large research laboratory of an American corporation, the director walks around and asks a single question of each scientist, "Are you having fun?" He feels that if his employees are having fun, that is, finding pleasure in their research, then great things will happen. The same is true with us. If our work is to be prayer and nourish us, then it will be fun . . . it will be pleasure. If we cannot find pleasure in what we do, we should perhaps change our attitudes or change our work.

If we enjoy our work, find fun in the challenge of it, we will no doubt do a good job. Excellence will be the result. Today, when so many of the products that we buy break down, we cannot but wonder if the people who made them found joy in their work. The loss of both excellence and a sense of pride is directly related to the loss of enjoyment in work.

The ancient Hindu and Christian method of liberation from attachment to things was to "offer to God the success or failure, the fruit of our labors." When this sacrificial gift has been given, we can enjoy the very act of work instead of its completion. It is much like swimming. The primary purpose of swimming is not to travel to the other side of the pool or lake, though that might be the case in some isolated occasion. The purpose of swimming is in the act of swimming. We find pleasure in getting wet, splashing around in water, one of the four sacred elements—earth, air, fire and water. We find pleasure in the exercise of our muscles, in the challenge of movement through water. So it should be in our work, when it is done in a sense of harmony. We find pleasure and prayer in our daily tasks, even cleaning our homes or preparing meals. Indeed we will find times when our work is unpleasant and even difficult. Since we are still in the process of regaining the harmony lost by Adam in the Fall, we must be patient with ourselves at such times.

A hundred jobs will cry out to be completed and

the clock may shout that we have precious little time left, but if we can discipline ourselves to stop and sit still each day—in a time of silent prayer or meditation—we will learn the patience and the spirit of harmony necessary to "pray always." Insofar as we are able to practice this simple prayer of daily stillness, of sitting still for fifteen or twenty minutes, we will soon know what is important among all the tasks that face us. We will "know" that what is important is our relationship with God, with ourselves and with one another. We will then balance our work between what is truly important and primary with that which is fun.

Then we are able to rise above the guilt-producing judgments of others and also our own guilt feelings about work; we will find a life that can be lived wholly and joyfully in the present moment. It will be a life lived as a gift from God. The reward will be a new set of eyes and ears. We will also experience the privilege of enjoying our work, something that is becoming increasingly rare these days. The Gospels tell us that the new Adam, Jesus, was a man who worked—that he was a carpenter. This work was not a preface to his ministry; it was a companion to his teaching and preaching. In Jesus we find the balance that Adam lost. For he had a profound awareness that his work was the Father's work and that he worked in constant communion with God. The words of Henry van Dyke so clearly express this:

This is the gospel of labor,
ring it, ye bells of the kirk!
The Lord of Love came down from above,

to live with the men who work;
This is the rose that He planted,
here in the thorn-curst soil;
Heaven is blest with perfect rest,
but the blessing of Earth is toil.

Jesus as a son of Adam and a Son of God was a contemplative. We should strive to be the same. As we strive to make our work and all we do think and feel a communion with the divine, we will find to our surprise that we are "praying always."

Simple Emptiness

As persons living in a complex society, we are aware that our lives are filled with numbers: our car license number, house number, telephone numbers, credit card numbers, social security number, health plan, insurance policy and zip code number. These and other such numbers are so much a part of our lives that the knowledge of numbers is expected, even from pre-school children. So when we hear Jesus saying "My Father and I are one" (John 10:30) it is only natural that we think that Jesus' arithmetic leaves much to be desired. Even a pre-school child knows that one plus one equals two and not one. Yet this obvious math error is at the very center of contemplative prayer.

Arithmetic and the use of numbers that allow us to live with comfort in a highly complex society began thousands of years ago with people making marks on a stick or making knots in a string. That amazing invention of our day, the pocket calculator, allows us to perform difficult math problems in the very palm of our hand. That is where arithmetic began, in the hand. Primitive arithmetic was counting fingers and the primitive signs for numbers looked just like fingers held up straight, II, III, IIII. Even early arithmetic terms for groups of numbers were but extensions of this system. The term hand meant the number five, two hands and a foot meant fifteen, and a whole man meant twenty. The Roman system for numbers, so simple and easy to learn, remained in use until almost the year 1000. At that time, it was replaced by the Arabic numbers that we use today. But before that date, both the Roman numbers and the Arabic numbers lacked an important number. This important but new number would come to Europe from India, traveling along the trade routes through Persia. This newcomer appeared about the eighth or ninth century in India and from there made its way to Europe. That number was zero. It must have taken a genius to have conceived such a sign since it was a symbol for nothing! In ancient India and China it was a sacred sign because it was the symbol of God, the absolute being. This sacred sign, the zero, was called "the Sunyata." The cousin of the sunyata or zero was the "white space" found in oriental paintings. This unpainted area was called "Yohaku." As the equivalent of the zero, it represented the presence of God in whatever was depicted in the painting. Oriental paintings, unlike our Western paintings, leave large areas unpainted while we usually cover every inch of the canvas to the very edge of the border. White space and the zero are cousins in symbolism.

Though Jesus had knowledge of arithmetic, essential for any carpenter, he did not have knowledge of the zero. For the arithmetic number had not yet been conceived. However, Jesus did have a deep understanding of the principle of the Sunyata, the divine emptiness. Jesus' spirituality was what we could call zero spirituality. St. Paul refers to this divine zeroness when he wrote, "Let your bearing toward one another arise out of your life in Christ Jesus. For the divine nature was his from the first; yet he did not prize his equality but made himself nothing . . . (zero) . . . He humbled himself and in obedience accepted death, death upon a cross" (Phil. 2:5–9). Now, if Jesus had made himself into nothing, into a zero, we are able to understand his unique mathematics. The Father and he were one, if in that equation, Jesus is zero, for one plus zero does equal one!

Jesus emptied himself and became the perfect zero which acts like a mirror that reflects whatever is before it: $8 + 0 = 8$; $3 + 0 = 3$. St. Paul urges each of us in our daily dealings with one another to pattern ourselves upon this mathematical mysticism. Your needs and concerns are perfectly mirrored in me as I attempt to zero my needs in order to serve you. But who wants to be a zero, a nothing, a nobody who is some sort of cipher in society? Our entire education and formation, if not motivation, are directed towards the becoming of a "somebody." Who would be interested in becoming a disciple of a zero, even a divine zero? Yet to be a zero is not to become a nothing, for as the 14th century German Mystic, Master Eckhart, said, "A flea, as it is in God, ranks above the highest angel in itself. Thus, in God, all things are equal and are God himself. True poverty of spirit requires that a man shall be emptied of God and all his works, so that if God wants to act in the soul, he himself must be the place in which he acts!" To be emptied of God and his holy things seems to be a religious contradiction; yet in this zero spirituality we find the doorway to contemplative union with God. We find that in such a mirror state, we are not devoid of God or even of self, but rather that in such a humble and open state we have truly found what we seek. But perhaps a story will help to make this somewhat clearer.

The Chinese have a story about a rainmaker. There was this remote village in ancient China that had suffered from a long drought. The fields were parched and giant cracks jigsawed the earth. The harvest was all but doomed. The villagers facing sure starvation prayed to their ancestors and urged their temple priests to take the images of the gods from their shrines and to parade with them through the village and fields. All to no avail; regardless of the prayers and clouds of incense that ascended, no rain fell. So in despair, they sent off afar for a rainmaker. When the little old man arrived in the village, the elders asked him what he needed to effect his magic. The old man replied, "Nothing, only a quiet place where I can be alone." So he was given a little hut on the edge of the village where he did nothing but live a simple, quiet life, doing the ordinary things that are required in life. On the third day, the rains came!

Rainmakers are zero people and zero people are rainmakers. They go about their business without making a fuss or a fanfare. They are inconspicuous but their spirituality gives them power. Such people do not cause things to happen, but by their presence, that zero magic, they allow things to happen through them. Chinese rainmakers do not cause the rain by complex magic; they allow the rain to fall. Hustle and bustle are not part of their lives. Rather tranquility and harmony radiate out from within them. Wherever such people live, the rains come with their fertile powers that cause things to grow and life to appear. God shines through such people as sunlight shines through a donut. As it is said in the Book of the Tao, "Thirty spokes share the wheel's hub; it is the center hole that makes it useful. Shape clay into a vessel; it is the space within that makes it useful" (Tao, Chapter 11).

In prayer and in our life, we should strive to empty ourselves first of that which is not truly us. We zero out the false and artificial poses that so often pass for the real person. We attempt to be hollow of our own demands and overly selfish needs when others come to us for assistance. As we walk in nature, we empty the mind of its ever-constant concerns and intellectual activity so that we might mirror the flower or the lake and so enter into communion with it by becoming it! In our prayer, especially the prayer of meditation, we seek an emptiness that is but a mirror quality of the soul so that it might more perfectly reflect God. Such emptiness is not a void but rather a state of openness to receive and to be filled. Zero prayer is that constant striving to become like Eckhart's flea who was filled with God because it had been emptied of self. Zero spirituality is the living out of the special poverty of the saints which may or may not have to do with possessions or property since it is concern with the inner poverty or emptiness of the heart.

But such a style of spirituality is difficult, just as difficult as it is to be a true Chinese rainmaker and allow life to be, instead of making it be. All of us find white space difficult in our prayers and in our lives. We find it difficult to be quiet, to sit still without having to have "something going on." It all seems so unproductive. We are a people who enjoy filling our days and our prayers right up to the edge with activity. As a result, there is little if any room left for the *Yohaku*, that empty space, that allows the divine mystery to be in the picture! Our prayers and worship reflect our overly busy lives instead of reflecting the divine. So we should not be surprised at the lack of tranquility in our daily lives.

We should not be ashamed that we find the task of creating white space, that area devoid of activity and productive thought, difficult. For it is hard work and calls for effort and discipline. An old Chinese master painter was asked about one of his great masterpieces. The painting was a giant scroll depicting a mountain with a forest, a large lake with a tea house on an island, fishermen, birds, and a gentle mist rising from the lake. He was asked, "What was the most difficult part of that painting for you?" And the old master replied, "The most difficult part was the unpainted area."

So for us as well, in our prayers and in our lifestyle, the most difficult part will be creating space for the unspoken and the unthought. While being difficult, this contemplative prayer of being one with God, one with whatever or whoever is before us, is in reality so simple. We have only to empty ourselves to be full. But we need to be reminded of that simple necessity and perhaps here is where we can return to our beginning reflection on the importance of numbers in our daily life. Perhaps the next time you see a zero, in a telephone number or on a license tag, you can look at that zero and see it as a sacred sign. The zero can be a holy reminder to put some zero space into your prayer and life. Each time I write our zip code, 66020, I write a sacred sign and remind myself once again to seek that mystical union that Jesus spoke of when he said, "I pray . . . that they may be one, as we are one; I in them and thou in me, may they be perfectly one" (John 17:23). May the zero, pilgrim number from India, hold the key to the divine door. I would like to close with a short tale from the Moslem mystic sufi tradition:

One went to the door of the Beloved and knocked. A voice answered: "Who is there?" He answered, "It is I." And the voice said, "There is no room here for me and thee." And the door remained shut. After a year of solitude and poverty this same man returned to the door of the Beloved and knocked. A voice from within asked: "Who is there?" And the man answered, "It is You." And the door opened unto him.

Complications of Simplicity

Certain words hold great charm for us and there are even some words that possess magical power, words like: discount, sale, 50% off, and reduced to go! Along with magical words, we have magical places that possess a magnetic power, places like: bargain shops, discount stores, garage sales, thrift shops, and the good, old-fashioned auction sale. The reason why these words and places hold such power over us is that we are a people who like to buy things. Most of all, we get a thrill out of buying things cheaply. Since we are a consumer society, consuming is an important part of our lifestyle. In former times people relaxed by sitting on the front porch and visiting, or even reading a book. Today recreation is frequently found by visiting shopping centers and the huge modern complex called the Shopping Mall. In the process of "just looking around," we find some item on sale. What joy in heaven or on earth can be compared to that of a person who bought something "for almost nothing!"

Poverty had an important place in the kingdom of Jesus as it did to the ancient Tao of China or the Gita of India. In all great spiritual traditions, simplicity or poverty is directly linked to prayer and holiness. In many traditions, poverty is a requirement for discipleship. Poverty, holy or otherwise, is an unpleasant word for our 20th century American ears. Most of us are middle-class people and for us that concept, "holy poverty," is a problem (for middle-class religious men and women it can also be a problem of guilt). The problem lies with memory. We remember the climb from economic poverty, the depression of the 1930's or the empty immigrant pockets of our families, and who wants to return to that again? As a result, our ears are closed to the words of the Gospel about poverty, the poor, and giving up all things for God.

The average middle-class family or single person lives so close to the bottom line with house payments, taxes, insurance, food, clothing, and the very necessities of life that little remains to be saved for the unexpected emergency. To talk about poverty or simplicity only complicates life. Yet, the words of Jesus and other spiritual masters were spoken to people who were truly poor. Two thousand years ago, there was no middle class, only the poor and the rich. The attitude of Jesus was simple: being rich was an obstacle to the kingdom of heaven. Jesus belonged to the lower class and never made any attempt to escape from that group of people. The attitude that he expressed was a positive approach to being poor. His requirement of giving everything to the poor and following him was not part of his general approach to all listeners. As a spiritual master, his concern was with dispossession and with simplicity as an avenue to wholeness and holiness.

Dispossession should begin with God! The first step is to renounce any possession of God by us who are mere creatures. God cannot be part of our real estate. Instead, it is we who belong to God and who should be possessed by the divine mystery. The first step then of any detachment is to give up ownership of God, and this is difficult for "church" people. Churches tend historically to want to possess "their" God. They attempt to keep this sacred possession secure by means of dogmas, creeds, rules, and a collection of rituals and symbols. They believe that such religious vaults will keep "their" God from being stolen or escaping. But just as you cannot keep a river in a bucket, so you can never possess the divine mystery.

The Christian theologian, Reinhold Niebuhr, warned against the substituting of religion or even Christian morality for God. He warned against hiding within the static structures of a religion instead of seeking the permanent revolution of the Kingdom. With Niebuhr we must ask whether the word "Christian" is a family name or a descriptive adjective. If we wish to use that name "Christian" as an adjective, then our thoughts, attitudes, lifestyles and values must be those of Christ. The difficult question of our times is whether our lifestyles can be the same as our society and still be that of Christ and the Gospel.

Poverty, dispossession and simplicity are truly alien terms to a consumer society. We are influenced by our environment, which is one of economic competition and consumption (interestingly, consumption is also the name of a disease that causes the body to waste away). The consumption of material goods is a value symbol of fulfillment and personal worth in our culture. The more you own, the more you are, is our culture's belief. In such a society, the main pursuit is that of the "good life," even at the heavy expense of nature and other people. To seek the "Good Life" is only natural, but to seek it in wrong places or in wrong ways is also destructive. Henry Thoreau challenges our concept of the "good life" when he wrote in *Walden*:

> Most of the luxuries, and many of the so-called comforts of life, are not only not indispensable, but positive hindrances to the elevation of mankind. With respect to luxuries and comforts, the wisest have ever lived a more simple and meager life than the poor. The ancient philosophers, Chinese, Hindu, Persian and Greek, were a class than which none has been poorer in outward riches, none so rich in the inward.

To live a life more meager than the poor is indeed alien advice to us. For us, poverty is not only outward destitution but inner destitution of spirit and life as well. But simplicity is to live a voluntary lifestyle that is outwardly simple so that it can be inwardly rich! Simplicity is a means to inner wealth.

Simplicity, as a spiritual tool and lifestyle, means the free shedding of possessions that hinder the development of the inner person. Simplicity means being dispossessed of those things that possess us (pause here and reflect upon what things you own and what things own you . . .). The former pious attitude towards spiritual poverty often seemed to imply that a person should be poor now so that one could be rich in the next life. Holiness is wholeness. Therefore, our lifestyles should contain a fullness of life today and in the life to come.

The simplicity of life will mean difficult things for different people. What brings inward richness to us will naturally vary with each individual. The question we must ask ourselves is not, what do we own or what do we not own, but does what we own add to our inner wealth? Do our possessions, great or small, keep us from being inwardly rich people? To one person, a piano may bring a deep quality of life, to another a collection of books or musical recordings will do the same. To another person, a tent or camper with which to be a part of nature adds to his inner treasure. Unless we, ourselves, know what it is that adds richness to our personalities, we will find it most difficult to practice simplicity. Instead we will follow the crowd chasing after the "good life" instead of investing in the richness of the inner life.

In Zen or Christianity, the great spiritual masters wisely did not set down any norms for simplicity. They only challenged us to make the dispossession equal to the value of life itself. To live in a simple way was a means to trust in the care of God. It was also a way to live in the present moment as you enjoyed all that was given as "daily bread." The spiritual masters tell a story about an old Zen monk and hermit who lived in great simplicity in a small hermitage in the mountains. One night robbers came to his hut in the forest and took all his simple belongings, even his clothes. As he stood at the window, naked, he looked out at the full moon rising above the treetops and said, "What a shame; I wish I could have also given them the moon!"

We who live today are not that different from people who lived in other ages. To seek wealth and luxury is natural. Examine any fairy tale or legend and you will find in it the search for gold and buried treasures. We instinctively seek life and we believe that luxury, which is the overflowing of good things, is but one of the conditions of such a good life. While sharing such a desire, we however, unlike previous ages, gather material goods with a consumptive appetite never seen before. Central to spiritual teachings is the warning that excessive consumption of material goods is an impediment to Life. We spend time, effort, and money and our talents almost without limit in our pursuit of the "good life," only to find that we have little energy left to seek the inner life. Simplicity is a revolutionary step of limiting the energy spent on consumption so that there is energy left for assumption. Assumption is that process of being lifted up, of reaching upward for a higher level of consciousness. Assumption is the result of meditation, prayer, and silence. It also results from the development of spiritual qualities by means of reading, writing, listening to music or poetry, gardening, jogging, yoga, cooking, story-telling and other creative activities. These, along with other humanizing experiences, increase our inner riches and lead naturally to an elevation of awareness. Assumption is the primal direction of all of creation.

As we find ways to increase our inner wealth, we will discover that the quality of our simple daily tasks will also increase as they become more enjoyable, more fun. Common tasks like eating, walking, doing the dishes or our work will begin to glow as these reflect the inner riches of our lives. This work of assumption does not require the purchase of a single tool—only the dispossession of anything that prevents us from finding time or energy to build our interior treasures. We can also be possessed by clocks and deadlines. Therefore, we need a simplicity of time so that we might truly know the difference between trash and treasure, between what is important and what is not. We need the wealth of time to develop a personal relationship with God, as well as a communal relationship that is expressed by some Sunday Worship. We need time to do the things we want to do, as well as the things we "have" to do. We need space and time to be free both in body and in spirit. Simplicity leads to leisure. Leisure leads to being peaceful, and peacefulness leads to the discovery that prayer is natural.

As always, the model for a lifestyle is right before us. As they say in the Orient, "A man in search of God is like a man riding his ox in search of his ox." The solution to our search for a pattern of simplicity is right in front of us—in nature. This concludes with a quotation from the rule of the community of Taizé in France. Taizé is a unique community composed of men from different Christian traditions living, working, and praying together in harmony. In their rule we find some excellent concluding thoughts on simplicity:

> The pooling of goods is total. The boldness to use the best way possible all present-day goods, without fearing possible poverty, to lay up no capital, give an incalculable strength. But if, like the children of Israel, you store for the morrow the bread that comes from heaven, if you work out projects for the future, you risk overtaxing the brothers whose vocation is to live in the present moment. Poverty is not a virtue in itself . . . the spirit of poverty does not consist in pursuing misery, but in setting everything in the simple beauty of creation.

Thanksgiving: Where Heaven and Earth Meet

In ancient Japan it is said that after a night of making love, the man had to write a poem so that when his lover awakened she might find the poem next to her sleeping mat. This ancient Japanese custom was intended to link together sensuality and love. The poem and the consideration behind its creation was a reassurance that the sexual exchange was a fruit of love and not just a "taking." The poem did not have to be a Longfellow epic. It could be a short three-lined Haiku poem like this one by Basho:

> As bell tones fade
> Blossom scents take up the ringing:
> Evening shade!

99

The thanksgiving gift of the poem was but one way to assure the woman that she was truly loved. Not only women, but men as well, need to be frequently reassured that they are loved. Expressions like that of the lover's poem, expressions that are both thanksgiving and affection, are essential to any human love affair. They are equally essential in our love affair with God.

The late Rabbi Heschel said that prayers of gratitude, blessing prayers, were the place where heaven and earth meet. A sort of nuptial union were these expressions that celebrated rainbows and God, new shoes and God, fresh bread and God, as well as the 10,000 other such "marriages" between heaven and earth. This sort of prayer-poem served the same purpose as the poem left by the Japanese lover. The Benedictions or short prayers of gratitude, as brief as a Haiku poem, were central to Jewish spirituality. If we, as followers of Jesus, seek to follow him, we would do well to explore this aspect of Jewish spirituality which he in his lifetime expressed so well. As Messianic Jews, persons with Judaic roots and traditions, but for whom the Messiah has come, we should seek the spirituality of Jesus instead of a spirituality about Jesus. A dynamic part of our tradition of prayer is the Berakhat prayers or as they are called, the Benedictions.

Catholic Christians among our readers are familiar with Benediction. Some may even ask, "What happened to Benediction?" Benediction was a popular devotion in which the Blessed Sacrament that had been placed into a golden sunburst vessel was adored. A blessing was given with the Sacred Body in the midst of a service of adoration and prayer. The service ended with the Divine Praises, a brief litany of praise and blessing that began with the words, "Blessed be God." With the coming of frequent reception of Holy Communion and the theology of the Second Vatican Council, the focus was changed from adoration of the Eucharist to the awareness of communion. The focus was not upon some "holy thing," but upon the mystical presence of God in the act of remembering, giving thanks, and in feasting upon the blood and body of Christ. As a result of this refocus of our attention upon the original intention of the sacred meal, the service of Benediction (once a weekly rite) became a rare experience. However, our need for adoration and gratitude did not disappear, nor did our need for that special style of prayer, the blessings. If the celebration of the Eucharist is to contain these expressions as well as the sense of communion with each other and God, we will need such expressions of adoration and thanksgiving in our personal and non-communal prayer lives.

The Catholic service of Benediction grew out of a 13th century worship need, but the prayer form of "Blessed be God" is much older than the thirteenth century. The Benediction prayer form was an ancient Jewish prayer form that was used by our Lord in his daily life. It was an important part of every meal and the Passover Meal as well. At the Last Supper, we know that "he took bread; saying the blessing, he broke it. . . ." The Berakhat prayers were the environmental prayer of Jesus, a spirituality that touched every aspect of his life. Scholars believe that these blessing prayers appeared about the fourth century B.C. and soon became an important part of the daily spirituality of the Jewish people. They were short prayers, no longer than a sentence or two. Their purpose was thanksgiving and an awareness of the Presence of the Divine Mystery in the most common aspects of life. An example of the benediction prayer used even today by the devout before eating bread is: "Blessed are you, Lord our God, king of the universe, who bring forth bread from the earth."

These prayers are not an act of blessing God, since only God can bless. They are expressions of proclaiming the holiness of God. Such prayers are acts of lifting up the spirit in gratitude for some particular gift. Berakhat prayers are so numerous that they touch each and every aspect of life. A brief review of them only reveals the poverty of our prayer-life today. For example, there are praise-thanksgiving prayers for each act of taste—special, different prayers for the taste of bread, wine, cakes, fruits, vegetables, ice cream, fish, and meat. Such an incarnational spirituality has prayers for the gift of smell, prayers for the special smell of the bark of trees, scented woods, perfume, incense, and fresh fruits. "Blessed are you, Lord our God, King of the Universe, who give a pleasant scent to apples." There are prayers for sounds such as thunder, for good news and for unpleasant or sorrowful news. There are prayers of gratitude upon seeing natural manifestations like rainbows, sunsets, lightning, stars, deserts, mountains, and trees blooming in the spring, and prayers for seeing a king or a scholar or a crippled person. In the case of the scholar, it is delightful: "Blessed are you, Lord our God, King of the Universe, who give of His Wisdom to flesh and blood." There are benedictions for touch, such as the brief prayer of gratitude for a new garment the first time that it has been worn, and there are prayers for anything new—a house, a pair of shoes, a book. There were also benedictions for each time that you washed your hands (always a religious deed done before you ate bread), and prayers said upon rising in the morning. These sunrise prayers of benedictions included wonder and gratitude for the gifts of sight, life, clothing to wear, and the ability to use one's arms and legs. These sunrise prayers were a sort of Japanese-Jewish love poem meant to reassure a love affair between the person and God. These were all expressions of the joyous thanksgiving of just being alive. This has been a brief and inadquate summary of a deeply religious custom, but enough of a review to reflect upon the presence or absence of gratitude and appreciation in our lives.

We live in a secular world, in the midst of a society that is non-spiritual, as well as not given to leaving poems on pillows. When we see a rainbow, we do not say "Berakhat . . . Blessed be God . . ." We rather say, "Wow, look at the rainbow!" Exclamations and slang like "Isn't that neat!" have replaced expressions of gratitude and praise. A few relics of a former age do remain. Usually people say a "blessing" before they eat and there is also the ritualistic toast with a glass of wine on a special occasion. Other than these occasions, we find a desert of devotion when it comes to a pause for prayer before the enjoyment of some common thing like a new pair of shoes. Even disregarding the absence of a spirit of prayer and the inability to live in the midst of wonder, we have also dulled our modern life so that we find little joy in just-being-alive. Instead of wonder and joy, our lives become a series of personal problems.

An ancient saying among the rabbis was, "A person who enjoys the pleasures of this world without a blessing is called a thief because the blessing is what causes the continuation of the divine flow into the world." The Japanese of olden times would have said the same. "A person who enjoys the pleasures of a woman without a poem is called a thief ... and a fool!" We are surrounded with love and wonder, encircled by marvel and beauty. To use these, to enjoy them without returning some expression is to be a thief and a fool. To receive any gift without an expression of joy and gratitude is to take something which is gift and treat it as non-gift. We rob ourselves, not God, by such arrogance because when we are unaware, the divine flow ceases. Gifts dry up like a Kansas creek in August. To live lives of gratitude by frequent actions of lifting up the human spirit to the Source of all gifts is to continue the divine flow of love into the world, your world and *the* world.

When Eucharist or thanksgiving is absent from our lives, the flow of divine energy ceases and our lives, as a result, become filled with troubles, trials, and stress. As a result, we begin to wonder about our love affair with God as does any person whose relationship with another is devoid of gratitude and poetic praise. We all need to be reassured and to be thanked. The classic Jewish Berakhat prayers were and are always in the present tense and that's important. "Blessed are you ... who create, who bring forth, who give. ..." To pronounce a blessing was to be reminded that the person was in the middle of the Divine Flow and that creation did not happen long ago, but rather that it is happening in the here and now! We can understand better Rabbi Heschel's statement that these benediction prayers are the place where heaven and earth meet, where God and clean hands meet, where God and fresh pears meet.

There is a story about a famous rabbi named Ben Zakkai who once asked his disciples a question. "Which is the worst quality a man should shun?" A student, Rabbi Simeon, responded. "One who borrows and does not repay!" Blessing or benediction prayers are expressions of gratitude for the continuous flow of gifts of smell, taste, sound, sight, touch, and a reminder that we are not the owners of earth, but only its guests. We are stewards that have been loaned a multitude of marvels. Life is loaned to us and we have been loaned to one another. Mindful of that non-permanency, how else can we respond but with gratitude? This Jewish concept of being aware that we live in debt for what has been loaned to us is also beautifully expressed by an ancient Aztec Indian prayer. This prayer from ancient Mexico, which also speaks of God's activity in the present, is addressed to God, whose name translated from Aztec means "He in whose juice all of us grow."

Oh, only for so short a time you have loaned us to each other. Because you take form in your act of drawing us, and we take life in your painting us, and we breathe in your singing us. But only for a short time you have loaned us to each other. Because even a drawing cut in crystalline obsidian fades. And even the green feathers, the crown feathers, of the questzal bird lose their color, and even the sounds of the waterfall die out in the dry season. So, we too, because only for a short while have you loaned us to each other.

Thanksgiving is not a once-a-year holiday. The Holy Eucharist is not some once-a-week ritual. Rather, thanksgiving is a way of life. Gratitude is the atmosphere that surrounds a person in love and is the environment for "natural" prayer. In our day-by-day lives we have the opportunity for 10,000 prayers. We need to find some modern and natural way to express gratitude and wonder. It might be of assistance to phrase our gratitude in some ritual form as are the Berakhat prayers. One could simply say, "Blessed be God who gives a parking place in front of the store." If a consciousness of gratitude is alive in our heart, a simple "'ahhh . . .'" could be a high prayer. Among the Sufis, the Moslem mystics, their name for Allah is "Ahhhhhhh."

As we reflect upon this prayerful expression, we should remember that the purpose of the blessing is not ceremony but gratitude. Ceremony is performed for others and is primarily external. These blessings are internal and are performed for the sake of God. The Benediction prayers are the turning of our attention towards God and are not to draw attention to ourselves. They are personal prayers and not an occasion to preach to others. These expressions are as personal as the love poem left by the Japanese lover. As such, they should reflect that sort of intimate personal relationship and not become bumper stickers.

Such prayers remind us that there is a difference between saying "thank you" and feeling thanks or gratitude. Prayers of gratitude tend to be intellectual when they come at the once-a-week ritual of the Eucharist. Benediction prayers, since they occur at the very moment of the experience, are directed towards what we are feeling. They are incarnational prayers that spring from the heart and not the head. They are love poems that are gifts of the moment and not debts of obligation.

As we reflect upon the numerous ways to be mindful of the divine flow, to be conscious of what has been loaned to us and awake to the 10,000 gifts of today, we will find ourselves with more gifts than we can unwrap. Among the multitude of gifts is one that is highly prized in today's world. Rare among us is the person who is satisfied. We seem to be constantly in need of something new, something different. Modern media have punctuated every aspect of life with commercials and their power to heighten our desires for new and better "things."

The by-product of the benediction prayers is the gift of appreciation of what we already have and who we are. That by-product also includes the results of the love poem left on the pillow by the Japanese lover. We know that God has made love with us and we with God.